Identifying and Interpreting Animal Bones

NUMBER EIGHTEEN

TEXAS A&M UNIVERSITY ANTHROPOLOGY SERIES

D. Gentry Steele, General Editor

SERIES ADVISORY BOARD

William Irons   *Erik Trinkaus*

Conrad Kottak   *Michael R. Waters*

James F. O'Connell   *Patty Jo Watson*

Harry J. Shafer

A list of titles in this series is available at the back of the book.

Identifying and Interpreting Animal Bones

A MANUAL

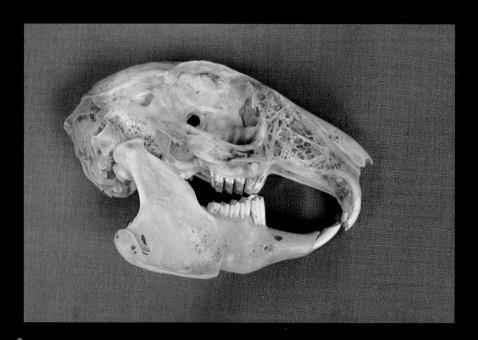

April M. Beisaw

TEXAS A&M UNIVERSITY PRESS
College Station

Library of Congress Cataloging-in-Publication Data

Beisaw, April M.
    Identifying and interpreting animal bones : a manual / April M. Beisaw.—1st ed.
        p. cm. — (Texas A&M University anthropology series ; no. 18)
    Includes bibliographical references and index.
    ISBN 978-1-62349-026-3 (flexbound (with flaps) : alk. paper)
    ISBN 978-1-62349-082-9 (e-book)
    1. Animal remains (Archaeology)—Handbooks, manuals, etc. 2. Animal remains
(Archaeology)—Identification—Handbooks, manuals, etc. 3. Archaeological
assemblages—Handbooks, manuals, etc. 4. Taphonomy—Handbooks, manuals, etc.
5. Archaeological surveying—Handbooks, manuals, etc. 6. Excavations (Archaeology)—
Recording—Handbooks, manuals, etc. I. Title. II. Series: Texas A&M University
anthropology series ; no. 18.
    CC79.5.A5B44 2013
    930.1'0285—dc23
                                    2013017719

Contents

Acknowledgments

I learned how to analyze and interpret animal bones from a variety of people, which is why my approach does not follow one school of thought. I was introduced to zooarchaeology while an undergraduate at Rutgers University. Robert Blumenschine and his graduate students provided formal instruction on African fauna. I picked up techniques for analyzing primates from Daniel Lieberman and for North American fauna from Cregg Madrigal and Sal Capaldo. Several faunal analysts served as instructors and guest lecturers at my field school on San Clemente Island, California. There I learned about marine species. While I was a graduate student at Binghamton University, Peter Stahl served as my MA and PhD advisor and taught me how to use animal bone data in creative ways while acknowledging its limitations. Philip Rightmire reinforced my knowledge of primate skeletal anatomy and Dawnie Steadman taught me the techniques specific to forensic anthropology. Various organizations have provided me with opportunities to analyze bones from archaeological sites across North America. Jill R. Hughes and David Zinn provided technical assistance with this manuscript. Several anonymous reviewers provided constructive feedback. My family, including my shipmates, provided me with the time and space to write.

Identifying and Interpreting Animal Bones

1 Introduction

The ability to identify animal bones from archaeological sites is a skill that few archaeologists develop without dedicated instruction in a classroom environment. In the absence of such a course, it is difficult to learn animal bone analysis, also known as **faunal analysis** or zooarchaeology. Most books on the topic can be either daunting in their coverage of the vast literature on method and theory or overly simplistic in their illustrations of complete bones of specific animals with little instruction on how to use them. What is missing are books that guide readers through the processes of comparing archaeological bones and bone fragments to known specimens or illustrations This book models the steps that an experienced analyst might follow, from receiving specimens to writing a basic report.

This manual should be used in conjunction with real animal skeletons, known as **comparative collections**, and books that illustrate the complete bones of specific species, known as **bone atlases**. For guidance on analyzing and interpreting the resulting data, books on zooarchaeological method and theory (e.g., Reitz and Wing 2008) should be consulted. Faunal analysis requires numerous resources, and the text identifies some "tools of the trade." A more detailed directory of resources is also available in the online appendix (see appendix 1).

Although readers can use this manual to identify a single bone fragment from any context, it is written specifically for those who wish to identify a large quantity of animal bone from an archaeological site. A collection of objects from an archaeological site is known as an **assemblage**. This term is not specific to animal bones. For example, the collection of stone tools from an archaeological site may be referred to as a lithic assemblage. It is common practice for animal bone to be separated from all other artifacts and for the bone assemblage to be provided to a single person, the faunal analyst, for identification and analysis.

Chapter 2, Preparing Your Assemblage, outlines the organizational steps to follow when an animal bone assemblage is received. Bones should be cleaned before they are sent to an analyst, but some additional cleaning is usually required. An initial sorting step reduces an intimidating pile of generic bone into smaller and more manageable piles of bones that share similar characteristics. This allows variability in the assemblage to become more obvious. Faunal analysis is all about pattern recognition. The first pattern an analyst should recognize is that of freshly broken bone, which may be mended to increase the identifiability of the assemblage as a whole.

Identification then proceeds in one of two directions: either toward the type of animal the bone came from first and then what bone it is or toward the type of bone first and then what animal it came from. In reality both processes are used simultaneously as analysts refine their identification. For example, a bone fragment may first be identified as a mammal bone, then a fragment of mammal femur, then as a white-tailed deer femur. To simplify this manual, instruction for identifying the type of animal is provided before that for identifying the type of bone simply because the former require fewer decisions. However, these chapters have been written so that they can be used in either order, depending on the analyst's needs.

Chapter 3, What Animal Is It?, provides keys for identifying the patterns that distinguish one animal skeleton from another. A basic knowledge of **taxonomy**, the organization of all living things based on similarities in their bodies and their behavior, is needed. The first question an analyst asks is, what taxonomic class (e.g., **Mammalia**, or mammal) of animal is this? This question can be answered by evaluating the texture, curvature, and thickness of the bone. The more specific the identification gets, the more knowledge is required. To discern what taxonomic order (e.g., **Carnivora**, or **carnivore**) or family (e.g., **Canidae**, or dogs and their relatives) the animal belongs to, an analyst must be able to recognize the patterns of **functional morphology**; the shape of an animal's bones are the result of how its bones function. For example, mammals that run fast often have fewer foot bones than mammals that do not; multiple foot bones that have fused make a more efficient runner. Functional morphology may or may not help an analyst discern the genus or species that a bone represents (e.g., *Canis lupus)*. To arrive at this level of specificity, the analyst needs an understanding of the species available to site inhabitants. Once a list of suspects has been compiled, comparative illustrations or specimens are used. If common species can be ruled out, more exotic species are considered. If a specimen cannot be identified below the level of taxonomic class, it is described using an estimated size of the animal within its class (e.g., medium mammal).

Chapter 4, What Bone Is It?, provides keys for recognizing patterns that distinguish one **skeletal element** (e.g., humerus or radius) from another. The easiest elements to identify are dealt with first, those of the head and those of the chest and abdomen (**thorax**). While fragments of these bones are readily apparent to a trained analyst, they are not easily identified to a particular genus or species. Teeth are the most identifiable element in the body, and in many cases a single tooth can be identified to the species level. Most animal bone assemblages are primarily composed of limb fragments. Techniques for discerning one type from another are described. For example, a fragment of mammal *long bone* that is triangular or D shaped in cross-section is almost always from a tibia or radius. After the bone is identified to a specific animal and element, the side of the body from which it comes can be determined. In some cases the sex and age of the animal can also be established.

Chapter 5, What Else Can the Bone Tell Me?, provides an overview of the taphonomic information that many bones contain. **Taphonomy** is the study of everything that happened to an animal from the time it died until it is described in a technical report. Some taphonomic processes leave marks on bones that can be identified and interpreted. Examples include bone broken for the extraction of marrow, cut for the removal of flesh, burned as part of cooking or trash disposal, weathered from long-term exposure to the elements, gnawed on by carnivores or rodents, or shaped by humans into tools or ornaments. Some taphonomic processes destroy bones before they can be recovered through archaeology. To gauge the amount of bone destruction that has occurred, analysts can consider the density of the recovered bones and bone fragments. This allows for an estimation of how much destruction may have occurred and can help to answer questions such as "Did people at this site not eat fish?" or "Were all the fish bones destroyed by processes of trampling or animal gnawing?" For additional information on taphonomy, consult the volume *Vertebrate Taphonomy* by Lyman (1994).

Chapter 6, Recording Your Data, provides guidance on deciding what data to record and how to record it. Before **databases** became user friendly, analysts used tables of abbreviations to code their data. Databases no longer require codes, so it is largely up to the analysts to develop their own recording system.

Any two analysts can analyze the same assemblage and produce somewhat different data sets. Because animal taxonomy is hierarchical, a novice analyst can produce a database that is as **accurate** as one created by an expert yet not as **precise**. For example, a novice may identify a squirrel bone as a **Rodentia** (order) or a Sciuridae (family). Experience and an appropriate comparative collection may allow an expert to identify it as *Sciurus carolinensis* (genus and species). The novice's data are not wrong; they are just not as precise as the expert's. A more general identification is always preferable to guesswork. The same holds true for skeletal element identifications. A novice may refer to a fragment as *long bone,* whereas an expert may identify it as a *left femur.* Additional data recorded should include descriptions of the completeness of each element and which, if any, **articulations** (joints) are present. Bones should always be counted, but they may also be weighed as long as they are clean. The presence of taphonomic marks (e.g., cut marks) should be noted, and any additional information may be added to a "comments" field.

PRECISION VS. ACCURACY

- A *precise* identification is very specific but may not be correct. Species-level identification is very precise, whereas genus-level identification is less precise. Precision is useful only when the identification is accurate.
- An *accurate* identification is correct, but it may not be very specific. A genus-level identification may be less precise, but if there is any question as to which species is represented, it may be the most accurate identification possible.

Chapter 7, Presenting Your Data, covers the basic calculations that all faunal analysts should perform on their assemblages: **number of identified specimens (NISP)** and **minimum number of individuals (MNI)**. These calculations can be applied at multiple scales to allow for comparisons between different areas of the same site or for comparison between sites. While other faunal analysts will be most interested in your NISP and MNI numbers, nonspecialists will benefit from other ways of summarizing the assemblage composition. **Body-part profiles** are one such technique. These drawings illustrate which bones of a specific type of animal were identified. For other ways to quantify and present your data, consult *Zooarchaeology* by Reitz and Wing (2008) and *Quantitative Paleozoology* by Lyman (2008).

Some general advice on preparing a faunal report is provided along with examples from actual archaeological sites. There is little standardization in animal bone analysis, and just one approach is presented here. Additional examples can be found in the online appendix (see appendix 1), which also contains photographic versions of all the bone images that appear here as line art (drawings) as well as some additional content.

This book is a manual and as such is not intended for a cover-to-cover read. Instead, select the chapter or section within a chapter that fits your needs at any given time during your analysis. If you need help deciding whether a bone fragment is that of a fish, skip to chapter 3. If you think you have a bone from a bird's wing, jump to the "Upper Limbs" section of chapter 4. If you are not sure what bone you have, browse through the figures until you see one that resembles it, and read the adjacent text for clues on how to identify that type of bone.

Animal bone analysis requires memorization of taxonomy and skeletal anatomy. Two features of this manual are designed to help with the tedious task of memorization. First, terms that every faunal analyst should know are defined in the text, and these definitions are also compiled into a glossary. The first instance of each term appears in "light" boldface type. Second, common and technical forms of taxonomic and anatomical terms are usually shown together throughout the manuscript to minimize the need to refer to the glossary while reading. To the expert, this may seem redundant. To the novice, it is likely a welcome teaching tool.

This manual does not contain bone illustrations in which each bone or bone feature is labeled with a corresponding technical name. Such figures are widely available in other books. Instead, the figures here allow the reader to examine the shapes of bones without distracting labels and to read corresponding textual descriptions of these shapes to enhance the three-dimensional visualization necessary for bone identification.

This brings us to some standards of taxonomy. The genus and species names of animals used in this book are provided in parentheses after the common name for that animal. Additionally, both genus and species names are italicized, and the genus name is capitalized whereas the species name is not. These are standards that you should adhere to. When reviewing lists of animals identified from other assemblages, you may see something like (*Gallus* sp.) or (cf. *Gallus gallus*). These are shorthand for tentative identifications. The former (sp.) means the specimen was identified to the genus *Gallus* but the species could not be discerned. The latter (cf.) means the specimen compares well with *Gallus gallus* but is not a perfect match. Some sources use *sp.* to represent "species" in the singular form and *spp.* to represent "species" in the plural. Therefore, if your specimen may be one of multiple species of *Gallus,* the correct identification would be *Gallus* spp. rather than *Gallus* sp.; however, this distinction is not uniformly applied in faunal analysis.

GENUS AND SPECIES NAMES
- Genus names are always capitalized.
- Species names are never capitalized.
- Genus and species names are always italicized.

When one genus name is used repeatedly, it is acceptable to abbreviate the genus using just its first letter in italics followed by a period (e.g., *Canis* sp. as *C.* sp.). To do so, the genus being abbreviated must be obvious from the context within which the abbreviation is used. For example, if you have written a paragraph about the species of the genus *Canis* and then a paragraph about those of the genus *Cervus,* any use of *C.* in a third paragraph would imply the genus *Cervus.* Because of the potential for confusion, use of the genus abbreviation should be minimal.

sp.—an unspecified species

spp.—multiple unspecified species

cf.—compares well with but is not a perfect match

C. (or any italicized capital letter followed by a period)—abbreviation
for the genus; use only if the same genus name was recently used.
For example, a set of *Canis* species can be written out as *Canis lupus,*
C. rufus, C. latrans.

Before identifying your bone specimen to a specific genus or species, it is necessary to determine what bone or skeletal element the specimen represents. The chapters that follow provide instruction on how to identify both complete and fragmentary remains. **Domestic** species contain a significant amount of skeletal variation. This is due to selective breeding and the creation of distinct breeds. There are more than eight hundred breeds of domestic cow and hundreds of breeds of domestic chicken *(Gallus gallus).* While your favorite bird bone atlas may illustrate the skeletal elements of the domestic *Gallus gallus,* the chances that your bone will perfectly match any chicken bone are small unless the breed of your bone specimen happens to match the breed of the illustrated bone. The same is not true for **wild** species. The bones of wild species often form near-perfect matches with atlas illustrations of wild species.

2 Preparing Your Assemblage

Although it is common for colleagues, friends, and strangers to thrust a bone at an analyst for on-the-spot identification and interpretation, faunal analysis is more nuanced than this. Of course, even an inexperienced analyst can provide general information about almost any presented specimen, but an accurate and precise identification usually requires a bit of lab work. Until you have a couple of years of analysis under your belt, avoid the temptation to perform such party tricks.

Bones should be provided to a faunal analyst only after they have undergone preliminary cleaning and quantification in the laboratory. At a minimum, bone should be dry-brushed to remove surface dirt and then bagged by **provenience**, the location from which the bone was recovered. Bone should not be presorted by field or lab technicians because incorrect identifications by non-specialists create many logistical problems in record keeping and hinder the faunal analyst's ability to recognize patterns in the collection. A paper inventory of the bagged bone that includes provenience and bone count should accompany the faunal assemblage when it is transferred to the analyst. This inventory can serve as an ordered checklist to guide analysis. It also provides the analyst with reliable typewritten provenience information, which is often easier to read than the handwritten tags that accompany artifact bags.

Faunal analysts should analyze their assemblage by provenience. Bones that were deposited together often have similar taphonomic histories; they may be parts of the same or similar animals or the remains of the same or similar activities. Therefore, each diagnostic (distinctive) fragment of bone can help identify another less diagnostic fragment from the same provenience. A provenience-based faunal analysis also allows the analyst to easily see the bigger picture of the assemblage. Each assemblage has its own characteristics, which combine to form a "personality." I call the discovery of this personality "becoming one with the assemblage." Spend a little time looking over the inventory and examining the contents of several of the larger and smaller bags before you begin your analysis. Getting to know your assemblage before reducing it to a spreadsheet of data can allow you to see its personality while you are still deciding what types of data to record (chapter 6). This will maximize the interpretive power of your database. Avoid the temptation to collect one type of information now and to collect additional information later on. Reanalyzing bones to collect new data that could—and should—have been collected earlier is time consuming and often leads to errors in **cataloging**.

Any given bag of bone will likely contain several similar specimens. Unless a unique identification number is provided for each and every bone fragment analyzed, it may be impossible to relocate a specific specimen to collect additional data at a later time. Unique ID numbers are useful but also quite time consuming, as each specimen must be labeled with its corresponding number, and the potential for typographical errors is very high. If unique identification numbers are desired, the work of assigning numbers and labeling bones should be completed before the assemblage is provided to the analyst.

There is no standard as to what data should be recorded for each bone during faunal analysis. At a minimum, all analysts should record the skeletal element (name of the identified bone) (chapter 4) and the **taxonomic group**, or type of animal, from which it came (chapter 3). You may also want to record (chapter 5) many other types of information, but trained analysts never overreach their abilities just for the sake of completeness. It is better to produce a very basic inventory of your assemblage than to misrepresent the assemblage with guesswork (chapter 6). For this reason you will find advice on recording data spread throughout this manual.

At this point you should have one or more bags of bone available for your analysis and a basic inventory in the form of a bag checklist ordered by provenience. For each unit or feature, organize the bags of bone by provenience with the first layers of soil removed, usually referred to as **stratum** one, ahead of the last layers of soil removed. Open the first bag of bones, and dump the contents of the bag onto a shallow tray. Be sure to keep a bag tag or the bag itself with the tray so that the bones do not get separated from their provenience information.

> **TOOLS OF THE TRADE**
> Plastic or metal trays greater than 8" × 11"—available at neighborhood discount stores

CLEANING BONES

There are two schools of thought when it comes to the cleaning of bones by lab technicians. One approach is to dump all bones into water and scrub them inside and out to remove all dirt. Fragile bones will not survive this type of treatment. The other approach is to treat all bone as extremely fragile and just lightly dry-brush the bone surface. Although this helps to preserve fragile bones, the amount of dirt that continues to adhere to the surface or fill the depressions and the marrow cavity can have a significant impact on the identification and interpretation of bones. Faunal analysts are masters at pattern recognition. One must be able to see subtle differences in order to make accurate and precise identifications and to recognize taphonomic signatures, such as surface cut marks that reveal butchery patterns (chapter 5). Since it is highly unlikely that lab techs will get better at cleaning bones, faunal analyst should be prepared to do some cleaning to ensure the quality of their own work.

Bone is porous and absorbs water easily. For this reason, I discourage analysts from using water to perform cleaning touch-ups once their analysis has begun. Wet bone cannot be returned to the bag from which it came until it is completely dry; if it is, it may develop a mold that softens and ultimately destroys the bone. The analyst's time is better spent analyzing than washing specimens and waiting for them to dry. Therefore, analysts need only to arm themselves with a few simple tools for bone cleaning. Surface dirt is easily removed with a denture brush, a larger and stiffer alternative to the toothbrush. Dirt that is packed into depressions or marrow cavities is best removed with an assortment of dental picks. Avoid the sharp picks; they will produce scratches on the bone surface. The dull-ended picks are strong and small and can tackle most jobs. A 10× magnification loupe or hand lens is handy for examining your cleaning progress.

> **TOOLS OF THE TRADE**
> Denture brush—available at neighborhood discount stores
> Dental picks—available from science supply companies
> 10× magnifying loupe—available from science supply companies

Cleaning should never damage the bones. If you are creating scratches or fresh breaks, then you have gone too far. The goal is to reveal structures that may aid in identification, not to produce a sanitary specimen. For example, the structures within marrow cavities can help to distinguish small mammal bone from bird bone. Therefore, jamming a dental pick into a marrow cavity to scratch out every grain of soil may actually reduce your interpretive power. Be especially careful when cleaning thin-walled bone, such as bird bone, for it may fragment; you might also produce new depressions or cavities that can hinder your analysis.

SORTING BONES

Now that you have ensured that your specimens are clean, sort the bones by grouping similar fragments. Do not pile the bones; instead, lay them in straight lines so that each bone is completely visible and can be easily compared to those around it with a quick glance. Bones that are complete (not fragments of a larger bone) should be separated from bone fragments. Bones that are flat should be separated from those that have complex shapes. Bones that are similar in color should be grouped together and so forth.

The main goal of this preliminary sorting is to be able to see the range of variability in this bag of bones while reducing it to a clear set of variables. This technique is especially useful when dealing with large bags of bone (more than one hundred fragments), as these bags can seem quite daunting at first. The truth is, most bags of bone contain little variability regardless of the number of specimens they contain. As previously mentioned, bones that were deposited together are often parts of the same or similar animals or activities. Therefore, the range of animals and bones represented by the fragments in any bag is limited.

A secondary goal of the preliminary sort is to evaluate the degree of fragmentation present. By the time a set of bones has reached the faunal analyst, it has undergone several taphonomic transformations. Taphonomy is commonly defined as the "laws of burial." Think of taphonomy as everything that has happened to a single animal **carcass** (the body of a dead animal) from the time the animal was killed until the time a fragment of one of its bones wound up in your hand. At a minimum, the animal died, its body was buried, the flesh decomposed, an archaeologist removed the skeletal material from the ground, the specimens were bagged and transported to the lab, and the bag of bones was cleaned and inventoried before being transferred to the analyst. That each of these events occurred is not important; what matters is how each event may have affected the bone specimens that you have been provided with.

For example, let us consider the taphonomy of a cow that was killed for food. First, the animal's throat was cut, producing a small cut mark on the surface of one or more neck bones (**vertebrae**). Then the animal was butchered, producing cut marks at and around joints (**articulations**). The head was discarded at the butchery site, but the limbs were sold to one buyer, while the thorax was sold to another. The upper limbs were cut into steaks, with the bones left in, while the lower limbs had the meat stripped off the bone. The lower limbs were discarded at this secondary butchery site, while the bones of the upper limbs were dispersed to several households as the individual steaks were purchased. The thorax was processed at a third butchery site, where a series of T-bone steak and rib portions were cut, each of which was also purchased by several households. A hundred years later, one of these households underwent archaeological excavation that focused on a trash **midden** (a trash heap comprising several layers of garbage) discovered during new construction; a backhoe had destroyed some of this feature. Several fragments of cow bone were collected, but others fell through the screen and were left in the field. The lab technician washed the larger fragments of bone, but anything the lab tech could not easily pick up was discarded. The washed fragments were inventoried by provenience and transferred to the analyst. Although you may now have four fragments of cow rib, this is only a small part of what once was. Part of interpreting the assemblage depends on your ability to understand what those four fragments of cow rib represent.

Various processes shape each and every animal bone assemblage. First, **biotic** (biological) and cultural processes restrict the types of animals available at any given time and place. For example, if overhunting (cultural) or climate change (biotic) has eliminated all of one species from an environment, that species will not be present in faunal assemblages created later on. Of those animals that are available, only a few will be removed from the living population (**thanatic**, or "death brining," processes), and even fewer will be processed in a way that their bones become deposited in the ground (**perthotaxic** processes). Some of those deposited bones will not survive the natural (**taphic**) processes that work to break down bone.

NATURAL AND CULTURAL PROCESSES THAT BIAS BONE ASSEMBLAGES*

biotic and cultural—pertaining to animals available at a given time and place

thanatic—pertaining to individual animals removed from the available living population

perthotaxic—pertaining to skeletons of individual animals that are altered before being buried

taphic—pertaining to skeletons of individual animals that are altered after being buried

anataxic—pertaining to bones that were buried and may have been reexposed and subject to additional alteration

sullegic—pertaining to selective removal of bones from the soil by the researchers

trephic—pertaining to selective analysis and curation of the recovered bone

*(Clarke and Kietze 1967)

The final taphonomic processes include reexposing buried bones (**anataxic**), removing them from the soil (**sullegic**), and analyzing them in the lab (**trephic**). Each of these biasing processes can be minimized through good archaeological decision making: where and how to dig; how the soils will be screened; what will be collected; the ability of screeners to differentiate bone from stone, ceramic, or the more common twig; and the ability of lab technicians to preserve the bones intact and to avoid additional breakage or unwarranted discard. It is the job of the faunal analyst to understand how these events have shaped the assemblage that you will analyze. You should always ask how the site was excavated and what was or was not collected. The abilities of the screeners and lab technicians are usually obvious from the amount of **nonbone** material that is included in bone bags.

If you are receiving a significant amount of nonbone material, you might want to pass on a few helpful hints to the field and lab supervisors. Bone is porous and therefore will stick to your tongue, whereas stone will not. For obvious reasons, this licking technique should be used only when absolutely necessary. Stone is usually heavier than bone and will produce a sharp sound when dropped on a table compared to the dull thump of a bone. Bone is usually more porous than ceramic, and therefore the lick or drop tests described earlier often work here, too. Some white ceramic material (e.g., kaolin pipes) is difficult to differentiate from bone that has been burned white, or **calcined**. Calcined bone is generally more fragile than white ceramic and can be scratched by a thumbnail. Bone is more resilient than plant material and therefore will not deform under mild pressure as plant material will. A twig will compress if you push on it with your thumbnail, whereas a bone will either resist the pressure or break. Use mild pressure, as this is all that is needed to deform plant material. Bone is also less buoyant than plant material and should not float on a water surface like plants do. Of course the buoyancy of bone depends on the presence or absence of air pockets within the bone or bone fragment. Be sure to fully dry any bone that is subject to the buoyancy test before placing it in a sealed bag.

SORTING BONE FROM NONBONE

bone vs. stone—Bone sticks to the tongue. Stone produces a sharp sound when dropped on a table.

bone vs. ceramic—Bone sticks to the tongue. A thumbnail can scratch calcined bone. Most ceramics will not stick to the tongue or be easily scratched.

bone vs. plant—Bone usually does not float. Plant material will compress if pushed on with a thumbnail.

MENDING FRESH BREAKS

Although most taphonomic processes can be accounted for only in a theoretical sense, a diligent faunal analyst can minimize one aspect of anataxic (reexposure of buried bone) and sullegic (removal of buried bone from soil) processes: bone breakage from archaeological recovery. Bone that was broken before it was deposited in the ground and bone that was fragmented while

Figure 2.1. Tray of bones sorted for mending of fresh breaks. Similar bones are placed together near the top and right of the tray, while bones with fresh breaks are lined up near the bottom and left of the tray. Fresh breaks are visible as brighter areas on the bone.

in the ground (e.g., trampled by animals) will be relatively uniform in color. Bone that has been broken during or after removal from the soil will exhibit a different color at the break surface. This is often termed a "clean break," as the freshly broken surface has not been exposed to the discoloration effects of the surrounding soil.

After performing the initial sort of bones, where bones of similar shape, size, and color are lined up near each other, examine each specimen for fresh or clean breaks. If any clean breaks are found, orient the specimen so that the break faces you, allowing full view of the break shape while quickly scanning the specimens in front of you. Move any specimens that lack clean breaks to another area of your tray while maintaining the organization of your preliminary sort (figure 2.1). This organization will allow you to look for breaks that can be mended or glued back together to recreate a larger fragment or even a whole bone.

The tray of bones pictured in figure 2.1 illustrates this sorting process. In the upper left corner of the tray are three mammal scapulas (scapulae). Moving clockwise along the perimeter, you will note teeth and cranial bones that contain teeth, foot bones and bones with epiphyses (see chapter 3), and a pile of long bone fragments without fresh breaks. The middle of the tray contains assorted bird bones to the right of the scapulae and a pile of mammal cranial bones adjacent to some fragments of vertebrae. The rest of the tray contains mammal bone with fresh breaks that are lined up in preparation for mending. The fresh breaks are oriented toward the bottom of the tray so that the shape of the break can be easily compared from one fragment to the next.

To identify potential clean-break matches, select one specimen, and then look for another that exhibits the mirror image of the break. To simplify this matching stage, place each specimen so that its interior surface is facing up. The interior surface is more indicative of bone structure and therefore more easily compared from one specimen to the next than is the exterior surface. When a potential match is found, place the freshly broken surfaces together. *Only perfect matches should be mended.* A perfect match usually results in near complete obliteration of the break when the two fragments are put together. If there is a gap or a missing piece, the match is not perfect and should not be mended without the missing pieces.

Once a perfect match has been found, place a small amount of paper glue along the clean break of one specimen. Try to use glue from a squeeze bottle. First squeeze out all of the air from the bottle while it is upright, and maintain the pressure on the bottle while turning it at an angle to squeeze out a thin line of glue. Once you have reached the end of the break, slowly retrace the path over the line of glue while slowly releasing pressure on the bottle. This will allow the bottle to suck up the excess glue, leaving a very thin line of glue at the break. Now the matched specimen can be adhered without a significant amount of excess glue being squeezed from the break surface. Wipe any excess glue away immediately with a clean finger, and hold the two fragments together with two hands for one to two minutes. Gently blowing on the mended area will expedite the drying process. Do not put the bone down or attempt to mend another fragment to the same specimen until the glue has dried; otherwise, the mend will deform. A deformed mend can prevent additional fragments from forming a perfect match on that bone because the shape of the bone has changed.

If it is absolutely necessary to release the bone before the glue has completely dried, be sure to set up a sandbox before you start the mending process. A sandbox can be made out of any shallow, clean container and a small amount of clean quartz sand. Fill the container with 1 to 3 inches of sand. The depth of the sand depends on the bone you need it to support. Deeper sand will be strong enough to hold a bone in almost any position necessary to prevent deformation of the mend. Be careful to avoid having mended surface anywhere near the sand; otherwise, the sand will become glued to your bone.

Mending bone takes quite a bit of patience, but the analyst will be rewarded with an assemblage that is both easier to analyze and more reflective of what was deposited in the ground. However, mending should not be overdone. Although you are likely to find fragments without clean breaks that clearly fit together, mending these bones will remove data from your assemblage, as these bones were likely broken by the culture that you are trying to learn about. I recommend using paper glue (such as Elmer's) for all bone mending, as it is water soluble and therefore completely reversible. If the patterns of bone breakage are of research interest, I recommend mending the bones with non-fresh breaks after the faunal analyst has cataloged the entire assemblage so that the original data are preserved before the reconstructions occur.

Once your bag of bones has been cleaned and sorted and clean breaks mended where possible, you are ready to begin identifying the specimens. Bones from archaeological sites are rarely complete. Therefore, the identification process outlined here focus on the characteristics that allow you to differentiate one fragment from the next.

PREPARATION CHECKLIST

1. Organize bags of animal bone by provenience.
2. Use an inventory of these bags and their provenience as a checklist.
3. Inspect the bones contained in several bags before beginning your analysis.
4. Use one or more metal or plastic trays to hold the bones of a single bag while analyzing them. Be sure to keep the provenience information with the bones by placing labels on or in each tray.
5. Use a denture brush and dull-tipped dental picks to remove dirt as needed.
6. Use a 10× magnification loupe to inspect the bone as needed.
7. Sort bones from a single bag by laying them out with the most similar ones together.
8. Remove any nonbone materials such as rocks, twigs, and fragments of ceramic; bag these separately as "nonbone"; be sure to preserve the provenience information.
9. Set up a sandbox for bone mending.
10. Inspect the bones for fresh breaks, and make any mends that are possible.

3 What Animal Is It?

All faunal analysts rely upon animal taxonomy, a hierarchical organization of the animal kingdom based on shared traits, to make their determinations. New research, especially in genetics, is constantly changing this ordering and hence taxonomic names. This is important because, depending on the source used (e.g., published bone atlases or comparative collections in your local museum), the same animal may be identified using a different name; for example, *Canis familiaris* and *Canis lupus familiaris* are both taxonomic names for the common domestic dog. Do not let taxonomy intimidate you. Once you become familiar with it, it will be one of your best resources for identifying and interpreting bones.

The University of Michigan hosts an exceptional Internet resource for animal taxonomy, called the Animal Diversity Web. This site provides a complete classification scheme for most species along with information on geographic distribution and wild or domesticated behavior. Pictures are provided for many species, and association of these images with a particular species is more reliable than images that can be found from an Internet search. Although years of faunal analysis will make you very knowledgeable about a wide range of animals, it will not make you an expert in identifying living specimens unless you take the time to consult such information.

TOOLS OF THE TRADE
Animal Diversity Web—http://animaldiversity.ummz .umich.edu

In taxonomy, the most specific level is species (and sometimes subspecies), and the most general is kingdom. Faunal analysis needs to begin at the most general level and proceed to the most specific if, and only if, an accurate identification can be made. Since this manual is about animals, we will be concerned only with the **kingdom Animalia**. Similarly, this manual is about bones, so we will be concerned only with the **phylum Chordata**. The next level, **class**, is where faunal analysis truly begins.

MAJOR TAXONOMIC LEVELS*

kingdom	Animalia = animal
phylum	Chordata = having a notochord (backbone)
class	Mammalia = mammal
order	Rodentia = rodent
family	Sciuridae = squirrel
genus	*Sciurus* = tree squirrel
species	*carolinensis* = eastern gray squirrel

* using the eastern gray squirrel as an example

CLASS: MAMMAL, FISH, BIRD, AMPHIBIAN, OR REPTILE?

This manual deals with the following classes: Mammalia (mammals), **Actinopterygii** (ray-finned fishes), **Sarcopterygii** (lobe-finned fishes), **Aves** (birds), **Amphibia** (amphibians), and **Reptilia** (reptiles). Each of the different animal classes has a skeletal system with unique features, which allows for relatively easy distinction. This is due to the importance of an animal's skeleton in enabling movement. For example, most birds fly; therefore, their bodies need to be as light as possible to minimize the energy required for flight. Most mammals, however, live on the ground and therefore need to be robust enough to absorb the stress impact of running, jumping, digging, and so on. If you compare the leg bones of a mammal and those of a bird of similar body size, you will notice that the bird has thinner-walled and lighter-weight bones than the mammal. This is functional morphology, meaning the function of a bone dictates its shape, and vice versa. Functional morphology accounts for most of the shape differences between bones that faunal analysts rely on for identification.

For ease of reference, some general characteristics of mammal, fish, bird, amphibian, and reptile bone are provided in table 3.1. These characteristics are generalizations, not a checklist. For example, while most bird bone contains some angular features (sharp points or complex projections), a bird humerus has no angular features and would be described as *rounded* (smooth projections). These descriptions are also relative. For example, if a bone weighs less than you would expect based simply on its size, it is probably not a mammal bone. *Glossy* refers to the exterior surface of the bone, and this can be influenced by taphonomic factors. In general, a mammal bone has a wood-grainlike exterior (figure 3.1), which is quite different from the naturally smooth bird bone. A translucent bone allows light to pass through it. If you hold a fish

Table 3.1. General characteristics of animal bone by taxonomic class

Class	Mammal	Fish	Bird
Weight	heavy	light	light
Glossy	no	yes	maybe
Translucent	no	semitranslucent	no
Shape	rounded	flat and angular	angular at some ends
Cortex	thick	N/A	thin
Spongy Bone	dense at ends	absent	thin support webs
Texture	woody	woody	smooth
Epiphyses	yes, fused in adults	no	cartilaginous in juveniles

Class	Amphibian	Reptile
Weight	very light	medium
Glossy	no	no
Translucent	no	no
Shape	rounded and angular	rounded
Cortex	thin	medium thickness
Spongy Bone	absent	present
Texture	smooth	woody to smooth
Epiphyses	cartilaginous caps may not fuse	cartilaginous in juveniles

Figure 3.1. Mammalian and bird bone with close-ups (50× magnification) of each showing the wood-grainlike exterior of mammalian bone (left) and the naturally smooth or lustrous surface of bird bone (right). These bones were recovered from a historic site in Maryland.

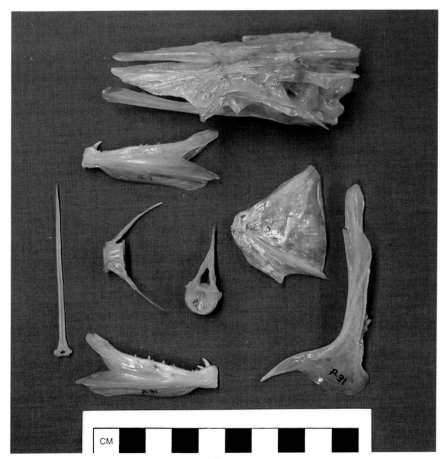

Figure 3.2. Fish bone *(Stizostedion vitreum)* showing translucent character.

bone up to a light, you may be able to see some light though it (figure 3.2), but this will never happen with a mammal bone. As described earlier, *shape* is the form of the bone. Mammal bone generally does not have sharp projections, but bird bone often does (figure 3.3). Amphibian long bones often have one rounded end and one somewhat angular end (figure 3.4). Amphibian and reptile bones often have very nondistinct articular ends when compared to mammals and birds (figure 3.5).

The **cortex** refers to the bone's exterior wall. The cortex of a bird bone is thin; that of a mammal bone is thick (figure 3.6). Fish bones are "flat" and have little space between their outer or inner surfaces. Within the cortex of mammal bone you may find **trabecular** or **spongy bone**, interior bone that is woven into a spongelike pattern. Spongy bone (figure 3.7) occurs at and near the articular ends of mammal **long bones** (e.g., humerus or femur) and throughout the interior of some other mammal bones. Dense spongy bone is almost always from a mammal. Bird bones do contain **trabeculae**, very thin deposits of trabecular bone that resemble a thin mesh, like that of a tennis

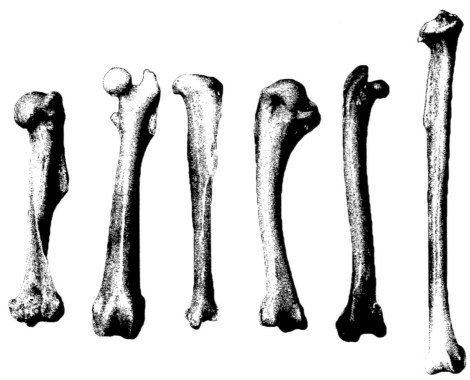

Figure 3.3. Long bones of a mammal (left) and a bird (right), showing more angularity at the ends of the bird femur and tibiotarsus when compared to the mammalian femur and tibia. The bones are from *Marmota monax* (humerus, femur, and tibia) and *Phasianus colchicus* (humerus, femur, and tibiotarsus).

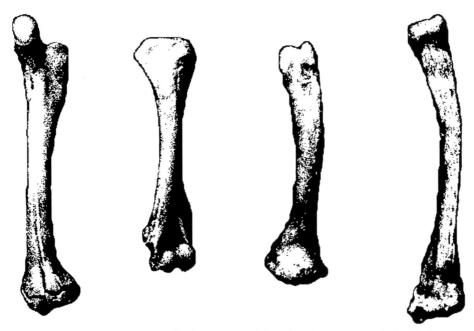

Figure 3.4. Long bones of a reptile (left) and an amphibian (right) showing the lack of definition of the articular ends when compared to mammals and birds. The bones are from *Varanus dumerilii* (femur and humerus) and *Bufo marinus* (humerus and femur).

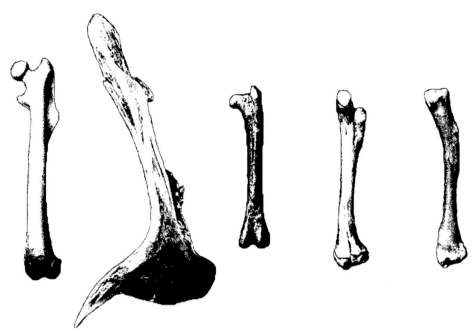

Figure 3.5. From left to right, examples of mammal *(Sciurus carolinensis)*, fish *(Stizostedion vitreum)*, bird *(Columba livia)*, reptile *(Varanus dumerilii)*, and amphibian *(Bufo marinus)* bones. The fish bone is a cleithrum (part of the shoulder girdle); all others are femurs.

racket. These "support webs" are densest at the articular ends (see figure 3.7) but also exist within the long bone cavities.

As animals grow, so do their bones. Mammal long bones grow at their ends, causing juvenile long bones to have distinct **epiphyses** (figure 3.8), or unfused caps, at their ends (more on this in chapter 4). Fish do not grow this way and therefore do not have epiphyses. Bird and reptile epiphyses are often more cartilage than bone. This cartilage **ossifies** (turns to bone) as the animal grows. In birds this ossification occurs at a very young age, and it is unusual to find a nonmammal epiphysis or juvenile bone in the archaeological record. An exception is sites where birds were raised for food and killed when relatively young. Even then, the cartilaginous ends of birds rarely survive the decomposition process, but their end-less long bones should. Amphibians also have cartilaginous long bone ends that ossify, but these bone "caps" remain separate from the bone into adulthood and often do survive in the archaeological record. These caps can be mistaken for plant matter, as they resemble a seed with a hole in one end.

Amphibian bones are generally quite long and thin and often seem "stretched out" (see figures 3.4 and 3.5). The reptiles exhibit quite a bit of variety from one order to the next. For example, the reptile order **Testudines** contains the turtles and tortoises, whose skeletal structure is very different

Figure 3.6. A broken bird (*Meleagris gallopavo*) bone and a sawn mammalian (*Bos taurus*) bone showing the much thicker cortex and denser spongy bone of mammalian bone (right).

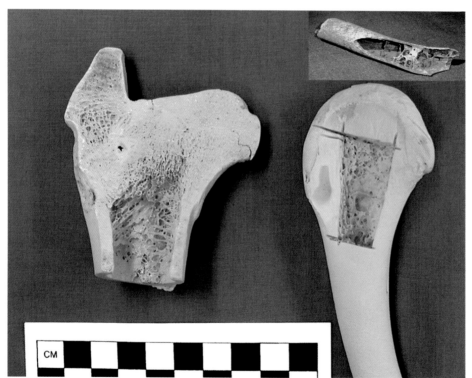

Figure 3.7. The interior of the articular ends of a mammalian femur (left) and a bird humerus (right) showing the difference in density of the spongy bone. The image in the top right corner shows the broken end of a bird humerus as recovered from an archaeological site in Maryland. Note the support webs and the thin cortex.

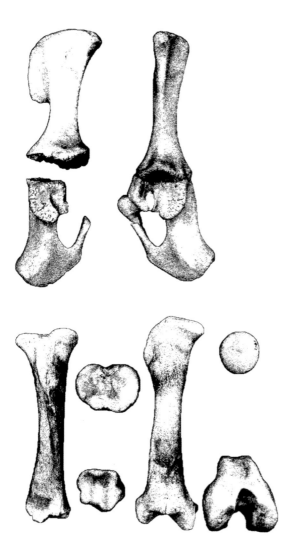

Figure 3.8. Examples of juvenile mammalian (Suidae) bone showing the areas where growth occurs. The innominate (top) is shown as separate bones (ischium and ilium) and as they will fuse (with the pubis). The tibia and femur (bottom, left and right) are shown with their epiphyses adjacent to them. Based on the lack of epiphyseal fusion, this pig was likely less than one year old when it died (Silver 1963).

from the reptile order **Squamata**, which includes both lizards and limbless snakes (figure 3.9 here).

ORDER AND FAMILY: A QUESTION OF FUNCTIONAL MORPHOLOGY

Now that you have determined what class of animal a bone fragment represents, the hard work begins. There are millions of species of animals. Fortunately, there are three major taxonomic groups between class and species: order, family, and genus. Just like with the different classes, each of these taxonomic groupings has its own corresponding bone characteristics that simplify the identification process. Luckily, not all taxonomic groups are equally

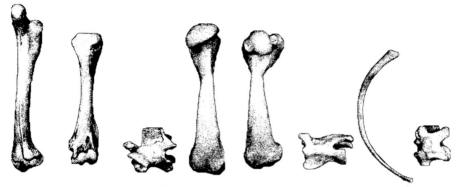

Figure 3.9. From left to right, lizard (*Varanus dumerilii*, femur, humerus, and vertebra), turtle (*Terrapene carolina*, femur, humerus, and vertebra), and snake (*Python regius*, rib and vertebra) bones showing the diversity of bone shapes that exist within the reptile class.

likely to end up in archaeological sites. Some are rarely used by humans, while others live in environments where humans do not. The following is a list of taxonomic orders that are usually represented in faunal assemblages. Having a good working knowledge of the present and past geographic distributions of taxonomic groups in your region of interest can quickly narrow down the list of potential matches for your specimens.

TAXONOMIC ORDERS COMMON TO ARCHAEOLOGICAL SITES

MAMMALS
Artiodactyla (artiodactyls)—deer, sheep, pigs, goats, and so on
Carnivora (carnivores)—dogs, cats, bears, skunks, and so on
Cingulata—armadillos
Didelphimorphia (American marsupials)—opossums
Lagomorpha (lagomorphs)—rabbits, hares, pikas
Perissodactyla (perissodactyls)—horses, donkeys, zebras
Primates—apes, monkeys, humans, and so on
Rodentia (rodents)—squirrels, rats, mice, and so on

FISH
Amiiformes—bowfins
Esociformes—mud minnows and pikes
Gadiformes—cod, halibut
Perciformes—bass, sunfish, perch, and so on
Salmoniformes—salmon, trout
Scorpaeniformes—rockfish
Semionotiformes—gars
Siluriformes—catfish

Anseriformes—ducks, geese, swans, and so on
Charadriiformes—gulls, puffins, and so on
Ciconiiformes—storks, herons, and so on
Columbiformes—pigeons
Falconiformes—eagles, falcons, vultures
Galliformes—pheasants, quails, and so on
Gaviiformes—loons
Gruiformes—cranes, coots, and so on
Passeriformes—crows, blackbirds, and so on
Pelicaniformes—boobies, cormorants, pelicans, and so on
Strigiformes—owls

AMPHIBIANS
Anura—frogs and toads
Caudata—salamanders

REPTILES
Crocodilia—crocodiles and alligators
Squamata—lizards and snakes
Testudines—turtles and tortoises

Species within the same taxonomic order have similar characteristics on a very general level, like dietary preference. For example, consider the following taxonomic orders: Carnivora (**carnivores**), Artiodactyla (even-toed **ungulates** or animals with hooves), Perissodactyla (odd-toed ungulates), and Rodentia (rodents). Each of these orders can be easily identified through their teeth, especially the **molars** (rear teeth) (figure 3.10).

Carnivora are carnivores in that their dietary preference is to consume animal tissue. Their teeth are adapted for eating meat, as they are sharp and pointed for grabbing and ripping meat. **Perissodactyla** are hoofed **herbivores**; their dietary preference is to consume plant tissue. Their teeth are adapted for grazing, as they may lack upper **incisors** (front teeth), so their top lip can grasp plants. Grazers also have small **canines**, if present, and their **premolars** and molars are tall and complex in shape to provide a grinding surface. Rodentia are gnawing herbivores, although some can be omnivorous. Adaptations for gnawing include large incisors without adjacent canines. The premolars and molars of rodents are flat and complex in shape for grinding. The order **Artiodactyla** includes herbivores and omnivores; therefore, there is some variation in their tooth form. Artiodactyla molars are generally more peaked than Perrisodactyla teeth for increased cutting surface; they are also not as square as Perrisodactyla teeth.

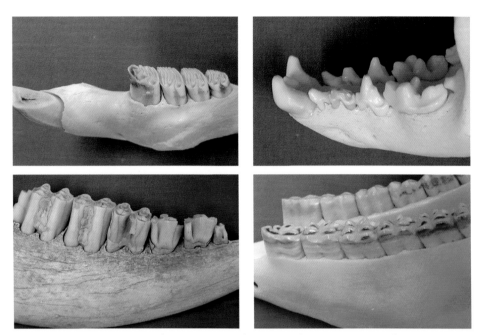

Figure 3.10. Molars of a rodent (Rodentia, top left), carnivore (Carnivora, top right), artiodactyl (Artiodactyla, bottom left), and perissodactyl (Perissodactyla, bottom right).

DIETARY PREFERENCE CATEGORIES AND TEETH

Carnivore—adapted to eat animal tissue; sharp and pointed incisors, canines, premolars, and molars; incisors are small.

Herbivore—adapted to eat plant tissue; grazers have small upper incisors and canines or lack them altogether; premolars and molars are flat and tall; gnawers have lower and upper incisors, no canines, flat and short molars.

Insectivore—adapted to eat insects; sharp and pointed incisors, canines, premolars, and molars; incisors are large.

Omnivore—adapted for both animal and plant tissue; incisors, canines, premolars, and molars, but none are very large or sharp; molars have lower peaks than carnivores but also have shallow valleys between the peaks.

As you can see, functional morphology is the key to determining which animals are represented in your assemblage. If you invest some time in studying living specimens to understand their behavior, your faunal analysis skills will improve. Teeth are especially useful as they can provide species-level identifications and age and sex determinations if the appropriate reference materials are available. Their density makes teeth more resistant to destruction than most bones, which ensures that most faunal assemblages contain at least a few teeth.

Each taxonomic order has its own set of skeletal traits that are the most useful for distinguishing between its families, genera, and species. The following sections present just a few examples for mammals, fish, birds, amphibians, and reptiles. As your expertise develops, you will notice skeletal traits that are useful for the animals of the region and time period that you work with.

Mammal Orders

In addition to dietary preferences, most mammal orders have very specific evolutionary histories and habitat preferences that can be used to aid identification. For example, Perissodactyla, a rather small taxonomic order, includes the families Equidae (horses, asses, and zebras), Tapiridae (tapirs), and Rhinocerotidae (rhinoceroses). A few things should become quite obvious from this list. First, Perissodactyls are native to the **Old World** (Europe, Asia, and Africa), at least during the human past. Therefore, if your assemblage comes from the **New World**, such as the American Southwest, and dates to A.D. 1000–1200, you can automatically cross all Perissodactyla off your list of possible taxonomic orders. If your assemblage does come from the Old World, you should be able to easily differentiate one of these families from another based on their body size.

Faunal analysts use the body size, or relative live body weight, of an animal to aid in identification. Once you have become familiar with the relative sizes of the skeletal elements of certain animals (e.g., mice, cats, dogs, deer, cows), it becomes fairly easy to estimate the size of the animal to which a bone belongs even without knowing its order, genus, or species. For example, rhinoceroses are very large and robust, and their bones are very broad or wide. In comparison, the bones of horses, asses, and zebras appear longer and much more slender. A large tapir can be the size of a small ass, but a tapir's legs are much shorter, and its bones are less slender.

Artiodactyla is a large taxonomic order and includes animals of various sizes that are native to both the New World and the Old. Artiodactyla is organized into ten families. Fortunately, most regions contain only a few of these families, and each family is quite distinct. Those commonly identified in North American faunal assemblages are **Suidae** (hogs and pigs), **Cervidae** (deer, elk, moose), **Bovidae** (bison, cows, sheep, and goats), and **Antilocapridae** (pronghorn antelopes). The families common to South American assemblages are Cervidae and **Camelidae** (camels, llamas, and vicunas). Faunal analysts who specialize in the Old World, especially Africa, need to become ungulate experts, as members of all families except Antilocapridae, **Moschidae** (musk deer), and **Tayassuidae** (peccaries) are found there.

When faced with large taxonomic orders like Artiodactyla, subcategories of the main taxonomic hierarchy become useful. For example, Artiodactyla can be broken down into suborders like **Ruminantia**. Members of Ruminantia

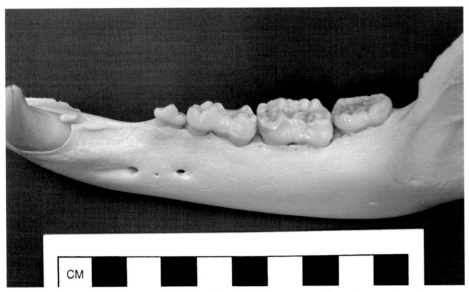

Figure 3.11. The mandible of a bear (Ursidae) showing the mixture of carnivore and omnivore traits. The molars are squarish with low crowns and many peaks (cusps) for processing a variety of foods. The canines are large and pointed for grabbing and ripping meat.

have specialized teeth and complex stomachs to process the large amounts of grass. Ruminantia teeth are **hypsodont** and **selenodont** (see artiodactyl and perissodactyl teeth in figure 3.10), high-crowned teeth with grinding surfaces composed of crescent-shaped ridges. The **crown** of a tooth is the enamel that is exposed above the jaw; high-crowned teeth are tall. In contrast, members of the suborder **Suinae** are more omnivorous and have **brachyodont** and **bunodont** teeth, wide and low-crowned teeth with rounded cusps on the grinding surface. Members of Suinae include pigs (family Suidae), peccaries (family Tayassuidae), and hippopotamuses (family Hippopotamidae). Within the Suinae, additional differences allow for differentiation. For example, each pig molar has a complex set of peaks and valleys for processing a wide range of foods. Therefore, a pig molar looks like a miniature mountain chain. Omnivores in other taxonomic groups have similar dental features. Although a member of the order Carnivora, bears (family **Ursidae**) are omnivorous and have brachyodont and bunodont molars that resemble those of pigs (figure 3.11).

MAMMAL TOOTH TYPES

brachyodont—wide and low crowned; characteristic of omnivores
hypsodont—high crowned; characteristic of herbivores
lophodont—having ridges between cusps; common in Rodentia
selenodont—having ridges that surround cusps; common in Artiodactyla
bunodont—having rounded cusps; common in Primates
secodont—bladelike teeth; common in Carnivora

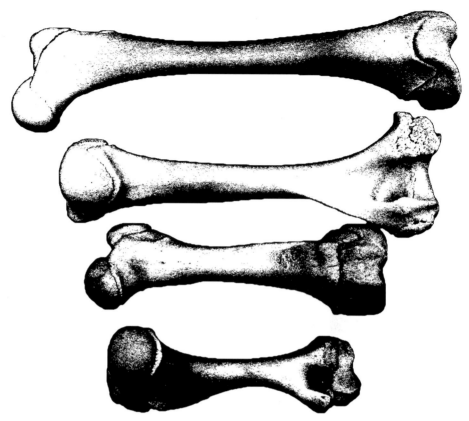

Figure 3.12. Bones of a bear (Ursidae, femur and humerus) compared to the bones of a pig (Suidae, femur and humerus). All bones shown are from juvenile animals, hence the lines showing partially fused epiphyses. The bear bones (top) are long and thin compared to the short, stocky, and more twisted pig bones below.

In addition to tooth shape, other factors that are useful in identifying bones of the family Suidae bring us back to body size and functional morphology. Pigs are short but robust and powerful animals. As a result, their bones appear excessively twisted when compared to any other species of mammal (figure 3.12). If you have a complete pig bone, it appears ugly to anyone who has an appreciation of the natural beauty of most mammal bones.

Another taxonomic subcategory, the subfamily, is useful for differentiating a large family group like the Bovidae. This family includes all cattle, antelope, sheep, and goats and is organized into seven subfamilies based mainly on the shape of their horns. Members of the subfamily **Bovinae** have spiral horns, **Cephalophinae** have small horns, **Hippotraginae** have ringed horns, **Caprinae** have rear-projecting short horns, and so on.

The order Rodentia is also large and complex, with more than two thousand species. Rodent species are highly specialized for their environments, which

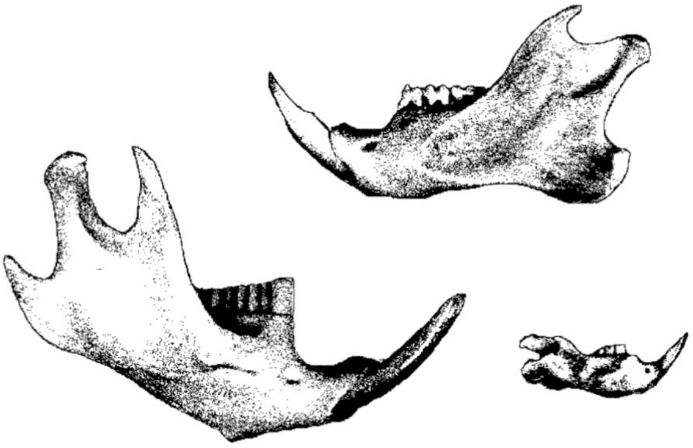

Figure 3.13. Examples of rodent mandibles, including a muskrat (*Ondatra zibethicus,* bottom left), a kangaroo rat (*Dipodomys* sp., bottom right), and an eastern fox squirrel (*Sciurus niger,* top center).

Figure 3.14. Mandibles of a jackrabbit (*Lepus* sp., left) and a desert cottontail rabbit (*Sylvilagus audubonii,* right).

makes them very important for archaeologists seeking information on past environments and environmental change. As previously mentioned, all rodents are gnawers and have long and robust incisors for this purpose. They also have fairly robust **mandibles** (lower jaw bones) to support these powerful teeth. Rodent mandibles (figure 3.13) are common in animal bone assemblages, and their distinctness allows for easy identification of each of the thirty Rodentia families.

Although many rodent species have relatively small bodies, their limbs are well adapted to their specific habitat and method of locomotion. Only one order can be easily confused with Rodentia, the **Lagomorpha** (hares, rabbits, and pikas) (figure 3.14). Lagomorpha is a very small order with only two families, **Ochotonidae** (pikas) and **Leporidae** (hares and rabbits). Some recognize a third family, **Prolagidae** (Mediterranean giant pikas). Pikas are not commonly recovered from North American archaeological sites, but hares and rabbits can be very common. All Leporidae are fast runners with long rear leg and foot bones that make them easily identifiable and distinct from Rodentia. Leporidae also have **skulls** (cranium and mandible) with many visible holes (**foramina** or **foramens**), especially on the **maxilla** (the upper part of the

Figure 3.15. A lagomorph *(Sylvilagus aquaticus)* skull showing the characteristic foramina.

jaw that is part of the cranium) and mandible (figure 3.15) and teeth that lack roots, causing them to become easily separated from their sockets. In contrast, the premolars and molars of rodents always have roots, but their incisors do not. Therefore, any small mammal mandible that is missing *all* of its teeth is likely a **lagomorph**. To be sure it is a lagomorph, you should inspect the tooth sockets. A lagomorph will exhibit just one deep hole for each tooth location. Multiple small holes for each tooth are indicative of tooth roots, and the animal is likely a rodent.

Once a rodent bone is identified at the order level, it is often easier to try to move to the genus and species levels than to attempt to determine which of the many families the bone represents. The same is true for most of the other taxonomic orders; exceptions include the order **Primates** (monkeys, apes, gibbons, and so on) and the order **Chiroptera** (bats). If you know that members of these orders were commonly exploited by humans in the region of your site, then you need to repeat the same exercise outlined earlier to determine which are the most reliable diagnostic elements of each group that is reflected in the skeletons of its members.

Fish Orders

Fish bones are a bit more difficult to identify than mammal bones for many reasons. First, there are more than forty taxonomic orders of bony fish (there are fewer than thirty orders of mammals). Second, functional morphology is not as useful with fish since the means of locomotion does not vary from one fish order to the next as much as it does in mammals. Third, the size of a fish body depends not only on species and age but also on the immediate environment. Fourth, the exact size and shape of bones and scales vary significantly throughout a single individual. Fifth, the complex shape of certain fish bones, especially cranial elements, makes it difficult to illustrate them in published bone atlases. Sixth, the size, shape, and fragility of some fish elements make them difficult to recover from archaeological sites, and therefore faunal analysts get little practice in identifying them. For these reasons, only specialists who have easy access to large comparative collections usually carry out fish-bone analysis. Those who do not have such access usually avoid identifying fish below taxonomic order or even class.

As with mammals, to narrow down taxonomic orders for consideration it is important to become knowledgeable about the types of fish available in the region and time period of interest, both freshwater and saltwater species. In the United States, regional information about current and past fish populations is available from the Department of Natural Resources. Disregard any species that were introduced to the area after the site was inhabited. Alternatively, you may consult faunal reports for other archaeological sites in the region to see what taxonomic groups have been identified previously. Keep in mind that preservation techniques can allow for long-distance trade, and therefore what is recovered may not fit your preconceived notions. On the other hand, preserved meat does not always contain bones, and therefore it can be consumed without leaving any archaeological traces.

Although similarities in the method of locomotion mean the shape and size of each fish bone is not as easily tied to a taxonomic group of fish as it is for mammals, there are several differences from one group to the next; as with the mammals, the most obvious is diet. The mouthparts of fish are specialized for the foods they eat and the method of ingestion. Some fish have no teeth, others have rows of teeth, and still others have plates of toothlike structures. Unfortunately, these elements are not well preserved in archaeological sites. In the case of tooth plates (figure 3.16) or **pharyngeal teeth** (teeth located within the throat of the fish instead of on the jaws), the plates themselves tend to lose their teeth and can be misidentified as fossilized plant matter.

Vertebrae are the most commonly recovered fish bones from most archaeological sites. One reason for this is that round vertebrae are more resistant to fragmentation than angular cranial elements and less likely to fall through

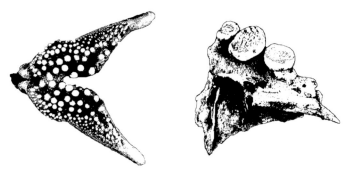

Figure 3.16. Tooth plate of a red drum (*Sciaenops ocellatus,* left) and a fragment of the pharyngeal teeth of an unidentified **Cyprinidae** (carps and minnows, right).

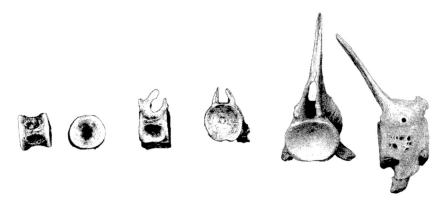

Figure 3.17. Vertebra from a salmon (Salmonidae, left), a carp (Cyprinidae, center), and a grouper (Serranidae, right). One side and one end view are shown for each.

screens than the long, thin fish **ribs**. In addition, most field and lab technicians recognize fish vertebrae and therefore are good at collecting and preserving them. Most fish vertebrae are not truly round; the actual shape can be diagnostic as can the degree of depression of the vertebral face, the size of the central hole or foramen, and the structure of the vertebral sidewall (figure 3.17).

Although mouthparts and vertebrae both show differences related to functional morphology, neither are as diagnostic as **otoliths** (ear stones found within the crania of bony fish) (figure 3.18) and scales. Both of these structures can provide species-level identifications of fish if an adequate comparative collection is used. Additionally, there are techniques to determine the age of individual fish using both otoliths and scales and to estimate live weights with otoliths (e.g., Hales and Reitz 1992; Morey, Klippel, and Manzano 1991; Monks 1981). Because of the difficulty in recovering these small structures, otolith analyses are not as common as they should be. Otoliths routinely fall through the screens during excavation, and field technicians who do not recognize them as faunal material often discard them. Although fish scales are

Figure 3.18. Otoliths of a freshwater drum *(Aplodinotus grunniens).*

more recognizable to a field crew, scales are very fragile and will survive to the analysis stage only if they receive special treatment by both field and lab staff.

There are four main types of fish scales, and they vary between taxonomic orders, three of which are discussed here. Members of the order **Semionoti-formes** (gars) have very thick diamond-shaped scales called **ganoid scales**. This scale type can also be found within the order **Acipenseriformes** (paddle-fish and sturgeons). The much thinner and fan-shaped scales are known as **cycloid scales**. Members of the order **Cypriniformes** (minnows and suckers) have cycloid scales. **Ctenoid scales** are more similar to cycloid scales than to ganoid scales but appear rounder in shape and have rear-facing pointed projections on one border. Members of the order **Perciformes** (perchlike fish) have ctenoid scales. Ctenoid and cycloid scales occur on species of other taxonomic orders as well, but compare any of them within your assemblage to Perciformes and Cypriniformes before considering other taxonomic groups.

MAJOR TYPES OF FISH SCALES
- ctenoid—round with pointed projections on one border; Perciformes (perchlike fish)
- cycloid—thin and fan shaped; Cypriniformes (minnows and suckers)
- ganoid—thick and diamond shaped; Semionotiformes (gars)

Bird Orders
There are approximately thirty taxonomic orders of birds, and although members of some bird orders have lost the ability to fly, the skeletons of all birds retain some flight-adapted architecture, especially the fusion of skeletal elements. Differences in the shape of bones from one species to the next is often more subtle than the differences found in mammals but less subtle than those found in fish. Unlike fish, birds tend to grow to a species-specific size despite their environment. Some degree of **sexual dimorphism** may be seen, as the males of bird groups can be significantly larger than the females.

Functional morphology is of limited use for differentiating birds because multiple taxonomic orders share similar lifeways. For example, **Gaviiformes** (loons and divers) and **Anseriformes** (ducks, geese, and swans) all live on the water, dive for food, and fly from one body of water to the next. Teeth are not useful in birds as they are in mammals and fish; hence, birds do not have teeth. Birds do have very distinctive heads, however, such as the relatively flat-faced order **Strigiformes** (owls) and the projecting-faced order of Anseriformes

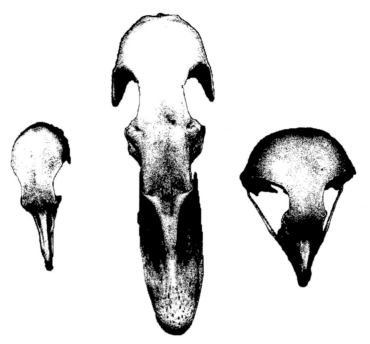

Figure 3.19. Examples of bird crania, including a pigeon (*Columba livia*, left), a duck (*Cairina moschata*, center), and an owl (*Otus asio*, right).

(figure 3.19). But the thin and fragile bones of bird crania make them unlikely to survive in archaeological contexts. Fragments of these crania are too small and thin for mending to be useful. An exception appears in the maxilla and **dentary** (mandible) of some birds, which are dense enough to be recovered and distinctive enough for easy identification.

Most differences in the postcranial skeleton of birds are relatively subtle, such as the curvature of the distal ulna in **Galliformes** (pheasants, quails, chickens). This trait is not easily distinguished from similar curvature in **Columbiformes** (doves and pigeons) without comparative specimens or a good bone atlas. When it comes to birds, it is best to identify the type of bone first and then compare a specimen to drawings in a bone atlas and/or actual comparative specimens in order to make an identification.

As with mammals and fish, faunal analysts should familiarize themselves with the range of bird species that are likely to have existed at and near the archaeological site in the relevant time period. When developing a list of potential bird species, remember to consider both residential and migratory species. **Residential species** are present in a geographic region all year, whereas **migratory species** live in different regions at different times of the year and pass through others. If present within a faunal assemblage, migratory birds can provide data on the **seasonality** (summer, winter, spring, autumn) of site occupation; therefore, it is important to identify them to the species level when possible.

The wild birds that are most common within our own neighborhoods today, **Passeriformes** (perching birds), are not commonly recovered from archaeological sites, as their bones are long and thin and fall through most excavation screens. The largest members of this taxonomic order, such as crows (*Corvus* sp.), are exceptions. As **commensals**, animals that share the same habitat as humans and benefit from that human occupation (usually for food), the significance of these common birds may lie in their ability to provide information about past environments and environmental change.

Amphibian Orders

There are only three taxonomic orders of amphibians, and only two of those are commonly recovered from archaeological sites. The **Anura** (frogs and toads) are more common than the **Caudata** (salamanders), although neither is as common as mammal, fish, or bird orders. The small size of most amphibians has kept them from being a significant source of meat for humans, and even when amphibian bones have become part of the archaeological record, they are difficult to recover without the use of dry column samples, wet screening, or flotation.

For those amphibian bones that are recovered, functional morphology is useful, as Caudata move on land or in water by undulating, while Anura rely mainly on their rear legs for propulsion. Because undulation is their method of locomotion, the vertebrae of Caudata resemble those of reptiles, specifically snakes (suborder **Serpentes**), more than Anura, whose vertebrae are somewhat mammal-like. The **pelvis** is the most common element of Anura recovered from archaeological sites. The musculature required for hopping makes the anuran pelvis both dense and distinctive. When recovered, a frog or toad pelvis is usually broken into three parts, but each part is still very diagnostic (figure 3.20).

Functional morphology is not as useful when it comes to the long bones of Anura and Caudata. For both, the long bones are relatively shapeless when compared to the long bones of mammals and birds. They are comparatively long and slender with gentle curves and little surface projections (see figure 3.20). Again, the small size of these bones makes them hard to recover but also makes them easy to identify as amphibian.

Reptile Orders

With new research on the relation of birds to dinosaurs, the taxonomic division between birds and reptiles has been breaking down. Many sources of taxonomic information, including the Animal Diversity Web, now list Aves

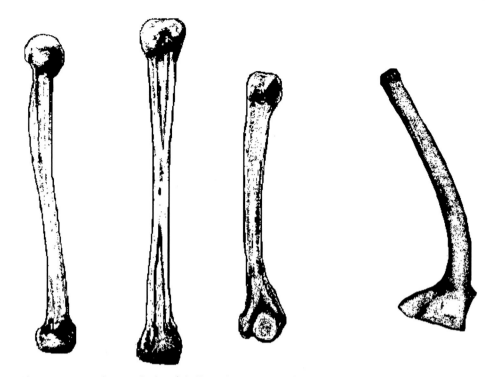

Figure 3.20. Long bones of a frog (*Phyllomedusa sauvagii,* femur, tibiofibula, and humerus) and the partial pelvis of a toad (*Bufo marinus,* right). Partial pelves of frogs and toads are commonly recovered from archaeological sites.

(birds) within the reptile order. Despite this new change, birds and reptiles will remain two distinct classes for the purpose of this manual. This is because the evolutionary changes that separated birds from other reptiles are reflected in their skeletons. Excluding birds from the reptile class, there are just four taxonomic orders of reptiles, only three of which are commonly encountered in archaeological assemblages. These are the **Crocodylia** (crocodiles and alligators), the Testudines (turtles and tortoises), and the Squamata (lizards and snakes). The skeletons of these taxonomic orders exhibit clear distinctions based on functional morphology.

Reptile teeth are somewhat useful for distinguishing one order from another, but since they do not vary in form (there are no incisors, canines, premolars, or molars), their usefulness is limited. The typical reptile tooth is cone shaped and is most similar to the shape of a mammal canine. Members of Crocodylia and Squamata have teeth (figure 3.21), but Testudines do not. Crocodylia teeth have roots that emerge from sockets within the jawbones. These are known as **thecodont** teeth. Some Squamata have thecodont teeth, while others have **acrodont** teeth, which are part of the jawbone itself, or **pleurodont** teeth, which emerge from a single common groove that runs along the jawbone. Without roots, acrodont teeth are not replaced when lost, and therefore the

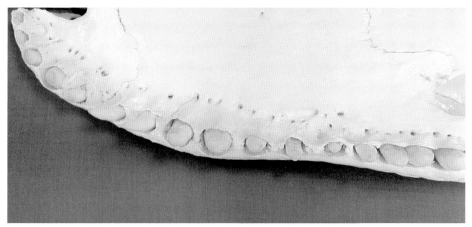

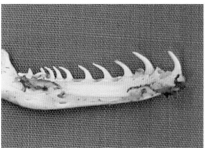
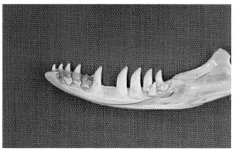

Figure 3.21. Reptile tooth types showing thecodont (top) teeth of a crocodile (Crocodylidae), acrodont (bottom, left) teeth of a snake (Boidae), and pleurodont (bottom, right) teeth of a monitor lizard (Varanidae). Note that the thecodont teeth are in individual sockets, the acrodont teeth are part of the jaw bone, and the pleurodont teeth are emerging from a single groove in the jaw bone, especially at the far right.

pattern of **dentition** (tooth counts and order) will vary from one specimen to another. Thecodont and pleurodont teeth can be replaced, but unlike the teeth of mammals, these reptile teeth can be replaced as many times as needed throughout the life of an individual reptile.

REPTILE TOOTH TYPES
- acrodont—having teeth that are part of the jawbone; certain snakes (Squamata)
- pleurodont—having teeth within a common root groove; certain lizards (Squamata)
- thecodont—having teeth with roots in individual sockets; crocodiles (Crocodylia)
- toothless—having no teeth; Testudines (turtles and tortoises)

Members of the order Testudines are toothless, but specialized skeletal structures that support their protective shells aid in their identification. The upper shell is called the **carapace**, and the lower shell is called the **plastron**. No other taxonomic group has anything similar. Both the carapace and the plastron are made up of interlocking plates that are unfused in juveniles. These plates may be found separately or in fragments within the archaeological record and can be mistaken for cranial fragments of fish or mammals. Look for a pattern of ridges on one of the two flat faces or a jagged but unbroken edge on one of the margins to confirm their identification as carapace or plastron fragments.

GENUS AND SPECIES: ENVIRONMENT AND ECONOMY

At the genus and species levels the identification of animal bones relies on the use of comparative specimens, comparative drawings or photos, and/or personal experience. Bone atlases depict the complete bones of various species. A selected list of such books is given in appendix 2. Although many of them are now out of print, they can often be obtained through a university library or purchased used.

> **TOOLS OF THE TRADE**
> Selection of bone atlases—see appendix 2 for recommendations.

Many bone atlases are organized in a similar fashion. The front of the atlas includes a labeled illustration of the skeleton of the taxonomic class the book deals with. Near this illustration is a list of illustrated species, including taxonomic and common names. This list is very important both to quickly determine whether the atlas illustrates the species that you may be looking for and to clear up contradictions in taxonomic names that are likely to arise. As discussed earlier in this chapter, taxonomy is constantly changing, and therefore older atlases are likely to use species names that differ from those in newer atlases. Many bone atlases also include charts near the back of the book that show the geographic distribution of illustrated species.

To minimize the number of illustrations they include, atlases depict only one bone for all paired elements (humerus, femur, and so on). For example, a left dog (*Canis familiaris* or *Canis lupus familiaris)* humerus will be depicted, but a right one will not. The standard is to illustrate lefts of all sided elements; the actual side shown is usually mentioned in the introduction to the atlas. Illustrations may be actual size or to scale. If no scale is provided for an illustration, you can assume that it depicts the actual size of the bone. Be careful when using photocopies of these atlases, as photo reduction or enlargement may have occurred. If a scale is provided, be sure to use it. These scales allow you to check the overall length and width of complete bones and the size of various diagnostic features. The easiest way to do this is with a sliding caliper.

To compare an actual bone specimen to a scaled illustration, place a portion of the illustrated bone between the stationary and the sliding arm of the caliper, and move the sliding arm until the caliper brackets the feature you want to measure. Now move the entire caliper to the measurement scale for that illustration and place the stationary arm at zero. Read the measurement from the scale, not the caliper, at the point where the sliding arm rests. This is the scaled size of that feature of the illustrated bone. Now move the sliding arm of your caliper to that measurement and hold the caliper up to that same feature on your specimen. If it fits, it is a match.

How close do measurements have to be to identify a match? Of course there will always be a slight difference in size between any two specimens. A good rule of thumb is that any two measurements must differ by less than 5 percent to be considered a match. For example, if the total length of an illustrated porcupine *(Erethizon dorsatum)* cranium is 100 millimeters, then the total length of the skull that is being compared to it must be between 95 and 105 millimeters for it to be a possible match.

TOOLS OF THE TRADE
Sliding calipers—available at your local hardware store or through science supply companies

---

The sequence of illustrations usually proceeds from the head of the animal to the tail; skulls and teeth are depicted first; vertebrae and ribs are next, if depicted at all; shoulder girdles (i.e., scapula) precede the upper limbs, pelvic girdles, and lower limbs. Hand (**manus**) and foot (**pes**) bones are rarely illustrated, but when they are, they appear near the back of the atlas. Vertebrae, ribs, and hand and foot bones are rarely illustrated because each individual has many of these elements, which also exhibit a great deal of variation in form within an individual (e.g., the first vertebra of the neck is very different from the last neck vertebra). Despite the significant variety, the differences in the morphology of these elements are rarely significant enough to make genus- and species-level identifications, which is the very reason for a bone atlas.

Bone atlases allow for quick comparison of an unidentified bone with multiple potential matches, but because of the limitations of depicting a three-dimensional bone in two dimensions, they can be difficult for novices to use. Therefore, a well-stocked collection of comparative specimens is the best resource for developing bone-identification skills. These collections require significant effort to create and maintain, but the exercise will improve your skills. Seeing an animal in each stage of the skeletonization process imparts a greater understanding of anatomy, butchery, and decomposition.

The biggest hurdle in creating a comparative collection is obtaining carcasses to skeletonize. An easy source of specimens is local road kill, but the diversity of species is limited. Once you have obtained both a **juvenile** and an **adult** and a male and female of any species, additional specimens are redundant. However, a few extra specimens of local species can be valuable as a resource to trade with other faunal analysts who do not have easy access to that species. Before building a comparative collection, contact your local government wildlife office to find out whether you need to apply for a permit to collect and/or possess wild species. The rules vary from place to place. In the United States, federal law does not allow the collection or possession of migratory birds (including their skeletons) without a permit.

> **TOOLS OF THE TRADE**
> Permits to collect road kill and migratory birds—if required by your local government

Once you have obtained a carcass, there are a few possible methods for skeletonizing it. The most sophisticated—and the most expensive—is to use a dermestid beetle colony. These flesh-eating creatures will remove soft tissue from bones quickly and easily, but the colony must be maintained, and unless you will be skeletonizing carcasses on a regular basis, this method can become costly. You must also ensure that the colony remains contained; many labs have fallen victim to infestations.

An alternative is to cook the carcass and remove the flesh manually. Depending on the age of the carcass, this can be a relatively malodorous approach, and the use of a fume hood, fan, or otherwise vented area is encouraged. One must also consider those who are downwind of such an activity. One faunal analyst is known for having covered a college campus with the stench of cooking skunk while he enjoyed a relatively odor-free lab space.

Another odoriferous option is to submerge the carcass in an outdoor container of water. The water and bacteria will skeletonize the carcass over time. Approximately half of the water will need to be changed periodically to facilitate the process, and small bones can easily be lost during these water changes.

The cleanest alternative is to let nature take its course by burying the carcass in soil. This method of decomposition requires patience, and the number of days or years required for complete skeletonization varies according to local environmental conditions. If you use this approach, be sure to bury the carcass deep enough to prevent scavengers from disturbing it but not so deep that the cooler temperatures of the earth retard the decomposition. A depth of 6 to 12 inches is recommended. You may also want to bury the carcass within some form of container to ensure the retrieval of small elements. This container should have some holes in it so that it does not prevent the movement of organisms or moisture through the soil. A mesh bag or wire cage is preferable.

Regardless of the method of skeletonization used, the resulting skeleton is likely to require some additional processing before it can be accessioned into your collection. Mammal and fish bone will require some form of degreasing; otherwise, your bones will retain a distinctive stench and be subject to mold growths and insect infestations. One way to degrease bone is to boil it, sometimes in soapy water. An alternative method is to soak the bone in diluted hydrogen peroxide. Caution must be taken to avoid overdrying the bone, which will make it brittle and subject to cracking (or worse). Some analysts also soak their bones in a preservative, such as a mixture of acetone and polyvinyl acetate, to help retain bone integrity and ward off mold and insects.

If creating your own comparative collection sounds like a daunting task, consider taking the time to identify a few museums and universities that will allow you to use their collections when necessary. Although these large collections are likely to have just what you need, it can be time consuming to wade through the specimens available to find what you are looking for. Virtual comparative collections are being built using three-dimensional scanners (e.g., Betts et al. 2010) and may prove useful in the future. For now, a happy medium would be to establish your own collection of those species that are common in archaeological assemblages in your geographic region of interest and save trips to larger collections for those specimens that are difficult to identify.

Once you have your bone atlases and comparative collections all lined up, it is time to identify your specimens. Functional morphology is still useful, but at the genus and species levels some common sense can expedite identification. Most animals end up in a faunal assemblage because they were part of the local environment or had economic value. Therefore, knowledge of the environment and economy of your region and time period of interest can lead you to a correct identification much faster than conducting a systematic search through bone atlases and comparative collections. After all, there is no reason to suspect that a bone fragment from a Native American site in North Carolina is from a dromedary camel *(Camelus dromedarius)*. Of course, with long-distance trade networks, nonlocal species can find their way into archaeological deposits, but you should always check local species before considering the exotic.

If your geographic region of interest contains a wide variety of habitat types, you can further narrow down the list of potential species by focusing on those that inhabit the area around your archaeological site. For example, mammals tend to be distributed by habitat type. Although some species occupy multiple habitats, it is possible to generate a list of mammals that are characteristic of the grassland habitats, where grass is the dominant vegetation and trees are sparse (savanna) or do not occur at all; forest habitats, where trees are dominant; mountain habitats, with their high elevations; swampland habitats, with their woody vegetation; or desert habitats, with low rainfall.

Appendix 3 contains lists of species by habitat type and definitions of each habitat type for North and South America. These lists are not exhaustive, but they do contain many of the species that are commonly identified in faunal assemblages. The lists are also useful when attempting environmental reconstructions. For example, if your archaeological site is currently located within grassland, but the species identified from the animal bone assemblage are mainly found on the forest list, it is possible that the local environment was quite different in the past. Alternatively, the inhabitants of your site may have exploited nearby forests. The difference between these two scenarios should be obvious from your assemblage. Although it is likely that a nearby forest was exploited for moose *(Alces americanus),* it is less likely that a hunter traveled some distance to obtain the Mexican wood rat *(Neotoma mexicana).*

Even though most archaeological sites do produce some wild species, historic sites tend to be dominated by domestic species. These animals represent the economic choices of the site's inhabitants and can provide a wealth of information. Do not restrict your list of potential species to dietary staples; cats and dogs are domestic species as well. We often get so focused on diet that we forget that animals serve other economic and noneconomic functions. In addition to live animals for labor or companionship, dead animals can be a resource. For example, some cultures rely on bone as a raw material for tools, ornaments, charms, or even building material. Although tools are usually made from readily available species, such as deer-bone awls or beaver-incisor engravers, ornaments and charms are often made from less common species, such as bear-canine necklaces. Begin your analysis with the common food species, but be ready to branch out to less common species and even exotic ones if necessary.

COMMON DOMESTICATED MAMMALS
Bos taurus, domestic cow
Capra hircus, domestic goat
Ovis aries, domestic sheep
Sus scrofa, wild boar/domestic pig
Canis lupus familiaris, domestic dog
Felis catus, domestic cat
Equus asinus, donkey or ass
Equus caballus, horse

Because animals are both environmental and economic indicators, another means of narrowing down the list of potential matches is to research what is already known about the cultural uses of animals in your region and time period of interest. Track down existing reports on the animals identified from nearby sites, and read up on ethnographic literature. The bulk of most archaeological assemblages represents the remains of just a few species. These assemblages are described as having low **richness**.

Low richness is common for economic and taphonomic reasons. Consider all of the species of animals that you have consumed in the past month. Many people have a list of favorite foods that form the bulk of their diet. My diet is heavy in turkey *(Meleagris gallopavo)*, chicken *(Gallus gallus)*, and salmon *(Salmo salar)*. Most of the turkey and salmon that I purchase are boneless meat cuts. This is not true of the chicken. An archaeological assemblage of my food remains would be heavily biased toward chicken. Therefore, along with the likelihood that a certain species may have been consumed, you need to consider the probability that its skeletal elements would find their way into an archaeological assemblage. Some animals tend to be butchered away from where they are consumed (e.g., steaks of beef), whereas others are cooked and served with little if any modification (e.g., pig roast).

4   What Bone Is It?

The real key to identifying animal bones lies in developing an ability to determine what bone you have, especially in the case of fragmentary remains. Let's begin with a review of the mammalian skeleton and the differences between mammalian and nonmammalian skeletons. Then we will cover some directional terminology that is used to describe both the location of bones and their features. Mammals form the bulk of most archaeological assemblages, and since humans are mammals, the bones of the mammalian skeleton (figure 4.1) are the easiest to remember.

The bones from the cranium to the pelvis are collectively referred to as the **axial skeleton**; they form the axis about which the limbs rotate. Beginning at the top of a mammalian skeleton, what is commonly called the skull is more accurately the **cranium** and the mandible. If the mandible is not present, technically you do not have a skull. The cranium is connected to the spinal column at the **cervical vertebrae**. In humans the first seven cervical vertebrae end at the start of the thorax, or rib cage, which includes the **ribs** and the **sternum**. Vertebrae that **articulate** with (touch) ribs are termed **thoracic vertebrae**, and a human has twelve of these. After the thoracic vertebrae are five **lumbar vertebrae**, the last of which articulates with the beginning of the pelvis. Nonhuman mammals can have different numbers of vertebrae, but most have about the same number of cervical, thoracic, and lumbar vertebrae as humans do.

The mammalian pelvis is actually made up of several bones, and here the variation in the number of bones increases from one mammal to another. The lumbar vertebrae articulate with one bone of the pelvis, the **sacrum**. The sacrum is actually a series of **sacral vertebrae** that have fused to form one structure. At the base of the sacrum are the **caudal vertebrae**. In humans the caudal vertebrae fuse to form the **coccyx**. In other mammalian species, caudal vertebrae may remain unfused and form the animal's tail. Sheep *(Ovis aries)* have seven caudal vertebrae, while pigs *(Sus scrofa)* can have as many as twenty-four. The sacrum also articulates with the **innominates**, or **os coxae**, which are each

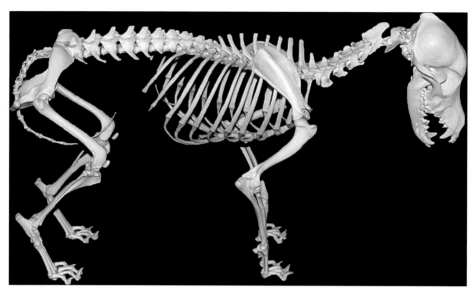

Figure 4.1. The skeleton of a mammal.

made up of the **ilium, ischium,** and **pubis.** (Most animal bone atlases use the term *innominate,* whereas human bone references never use this term.)

The limb bones are collectively referred to as the **appendicular skeleton,** or the appendages. The upper limb bones begin at the shoulder joint, or girdle, where the **clavicle, scapula,** and **humerus** articulate. The humerus also articulates with the **radius** and the **ulna,** which in turn articulate with the wrist bones, or **carpals.** Moving out from the carpals are the **metacarpals** and the **phalanges.** The number of bones present from the carpals on depends on the number of **digits,** or fingers, the animal possesses. The lower limb is similar to the upper limb. It begins with the **femur,** which articulates with the innominate and the **tibia.** The tibia is similar to the radius of the upper limb in that it is the larger of two articulating bones. Adjacent to the tibia is the much smaller **fibula.** Below the tibia and the fibula are the anklebones, or **tarsals.** Moving out from the tarsals are the **metatarsals** and the phalanges. Again, the number of these depends on how many digits (in this case toes) are present.

The names of the carpals and tarsals of mammals vary, as the wrist and ankle bones can combine in numerous ways based on the mode and speed of locomotion of the species and the dexterity of the hands (manus) and feet (pes). In addition, the names for the carpals and the tarsals of the human skeleton are not always the same in a nonhuman. A list of animal carpal and tarsal names and their human bone equivalents is provided in the following list.

TERMINOLOGY FOR CARPALS AND TARSALS
OF THE MAMMALIAN SKELETON

CARPALS
Radial = Scaphoid
Intermediate = Lunate
Ulnar = Cuneiform = Triquetral = Triquetrum
Accessory = Pisiform
First carpal = Trapezium
Second carpal = Trapezoid
Third carpal = Magnum = Capitate
Fourth carpal = Unciform = Hamate
Scapholunar = Fusion of scaphoid and lunate

TARSALS
Talus = Astragalus
Calcaneus = Calcaneum
Central = Navicular
First tarsal = First cuneiform
Second tarsal = Second cuneiform
Third tarsal = Third cuneiform
Fourth tarsal = Cuboid
Naviculocuboid = Fusion of navicular and cuboid

Now that we have covered the mammalian skeleton, an easy way to remember the skeletons of fish, birds, amphibians, and reptiles is to compare them to the more familiar mammalian skeleton.

The fish cranium, like the mammalian cranium, is made up of many individual bones that may or may not be fused to create a single structure (figure 4.2). Instead of a mandible, fish have a bone called the dentary, which may or may not have teeth. The cranium connects to the thoracic vertebrae, which are followed by the **precaudal** and caudal vertebrae. Both the shoulder and the pelvic girdles are found adjacent to the cranium since fish have fins instead of limbs. The shoulder girdle includes a clavicle and a **coracoid** along with several other bones with names that have no equivalent in the mammalian skeleton, like the cleithrum (see figure 3.5). In mammals the coracoid is just a **process**, a projection of bone that extends outward from the scapula. In fish, birds, reptiles, and amphibians the coracoid is usually a bone in its own right. The pelvic girdle is small and consists of a **basipterigium** and a few **spines**. Spines are long, thin projections of bone that occur throughout the fish skeleton.

While fish have more individual bones than most mammals do, birds tend to have fewer (figure 4.3) to provide a rigid body for flight. Like fish, birds have a

Figure 4.2. The skeleton of a fish.

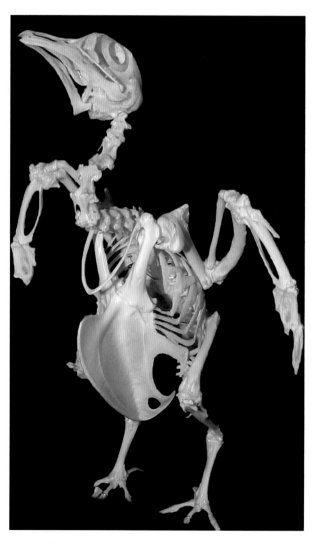

Figure 4.3. The skeleton of a bird.

dentary instead of a mandible. The cranium is connected to a column of cervical and thoracic vertebrae. Many of the thoracic, lumbar, sacral, and caudal vertebrae are fused to form the **synsacrum**, along with the ilium, ischium, and pubis (pelvic girdle). The remaining caudal vertebrae form the **pygostyle**, a series of fused vertebrae to which the bird's tail is attached. The shoulder girdle consists of a scapula, coracoid, humerus, and **furcula**. The furcula is commonly known as the wishbone and is the equivalent of the clavicle (or two fused clavicles) in the mammalian skeleton.

The bird humerus articulates with a radius and an ulna, which in turn articulate with the **carpometacarpus**. The carpometacarpus is equivalent to the carpals and metacarpals of mammals fused into one structure. Projecting from the carpometacarpus are several digits. The sternum, or breastbone, is usually very large, for this is where the wing muscles attach to the chest. The sternum articulates with the coracoid and the ribs. The pelvic girdle articulates with the femur, which in turn articulates with the **tibiotarsus** and the fibula. The tibiotarsus is equivalent to a tibia and some fused tarsal bones. It articulates with the **tarsometatarsus**, the fused equivalent of tarsals and metatarsals. The phalanges follow.

The amphibian skeleton also contains several fused bones. This skeleton (figure 4.4) begins with the cranium and the dentary. A few vertebrae are divided into three regions: the **presacral**, the sacral, and the **postsacral**. The

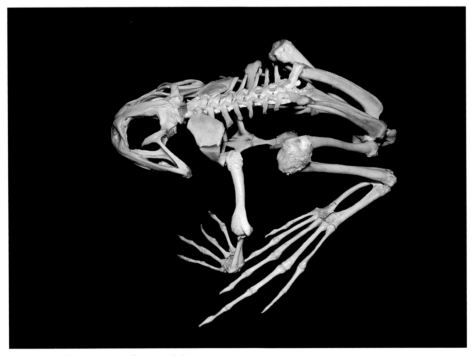

Figure 4.4. The skeleton of an amphibian.

shoulder girdle includes the scapula, clavicle, coracoid, and humerus. The humerus articulates with the **radio-ulna**, a radius fused to an ulna, which is followed by the carpals, metacarpals, and phalanges. The sacrum articulates with the pelvic girdle and the **urostyle** in Anura (frogs and toads). The pelvic girdle includes the fused ilium, ischium, and pubis. It articulates with the femur, which is followed by the **tibiofibula**, a tibia fused to a fibula, the tarsals, metatarsals, and phalanges.

The reptile skeleton is more variable in form. Snakes (suborder Serpentes) clearly lack limbs, and turtles and tortoises (Testudines) have a shell. A snake skeleton is made up mainly of a cranium, dentary, ribs, and a variety of vertebrae: cervical, dorsal, sacral, and caudal. The axial skeleton of a turtle (figure 4.5) consists of a cranium, dentary, and cervical and caudal vertebrae. The shell is made up of a carapace at the top and a plastron at the bottom. The shoulder girdle is composed of a coracoid, scapula, and humerus. The humerus articulates with a radius and an ulna, which are then followed by the carpals, metacarpals, and phalanges. The pelvic girdle consists of the fused ilium, ischium, and pubis. The femur articulates with the pelvis and to a tibia and a fibula, which are followed by tarsals, metatarsals, and phalanges.

When analyzing skeletons, you can use directional terms to specify the exact position of bones relative to each other. Two of the most important directional terms for any faunal analyst are **proximal** and **distal**. *Proximal* refers to a part of a body that is located toward the top and center of that body. *Distal* refers to a part that is located away from the top and center. For example, your upper arm is more proximal than your hand, and your fingers are more distal than your wrist. These same terms can be used when specifying a segment of one bone; most bones have two articulations: proximal and distal. The proximal end of a bone is usually quite different from the distal end in shape, and therefore it is important to be able to distinguish one from the other.

Other important directional terms are **medial** and **lateral**, **dorsal** and **ventral**, **cranial** and caudal, and **anterior** and **posterior**. *Medial* refers to the part of a body that is closer to the inside of the body (or the axial skeleton), while *lateral* refers to the part that is closer to the outside of a body. For example, the fibula is always lateral to the tibia. *Dorsal* refers to the part of a body that is above another part when the body is in its normal anatomical position. For example, the back of a dog is the dog's dorsal side. *Ventral* is a part that is below, such as the belly of a dog. These terms, *dorsal* and *ventral,* are used mainly for quadrupedal animals. For humans and other bipedal animals, *anterior* refers to the front of a body in its normal anatomical position, and *posterior* refers to the back of a body in its normal anatomical position. *Anterior* and *posterior* can also be used in general for anything that is toward the front or back. *Cranial* refers to a part of the body that is closer to the head of the animal, and *caudal* is a part that is closer to the tail.

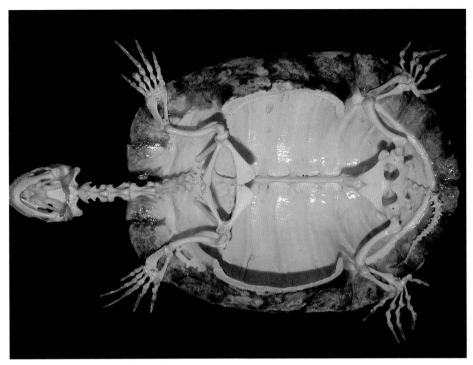

Figure 4.5. The skeleton of a reptile.

BASIC DIRECTIONAL TERMINOLOGY

Proximal—toward the top and center of a body

Distal—away from the top and center of a body

Medial—toward the inside of a body

Lateral—toward the outside of a body

Dorsal—a surface above

Ventral—a surface below

Cranial—toward the head

Caudal—toward the tail

Anterior—toward the front

Posterior—toward the back

Memorizing directional terms simplifies the analysis of animal bones, as many names and descriptions of bone features make use of them. Bone features or "landmarks" are very helpful in identifying bone fragments. For example, the distal tibia contains a landmark known as the **medial malleolus**, which forms the inside (medial portion) of the ankle. Once you learn to recognize its distinctive shape, you will be able to identify a tibia, determine its taxonomic group (e.g., Artiodactyl or *Odocoileus virginianus),* and **side** it (determine whether it is from the left or the right). To side a fragment of distal tibia, simply place the medial malleolus in proper anatomical position, facing downward, with the smoother anterior (front) side of the tibia facing forward (see "Lower Limbs," which appears later in this chapter). If the medial malleolus is on the left, it is from a right tibia because it is the medial or interior portion of the tibia.

SKULLS AND TEETH

A wealth of comparative illustrations and specimens are readily available to help you identify skulls, but skulls are rarely recovered from archaeological deposits outside of graves. As previously mentioned, a skull is actually a cranium and a mandible or a cranium and a dentary. The most diagnostic aspect of the cranium is the face or facial bones, yet these are also among the most fragile bones of the body and usually do not survive the processes of taphonomy. The more robust regions of the cranium are in and along the base or **basicranium**; however, this region of the skull is not often illustrated in bone atlases.

Fragments of cranial bone can be identified as such based on a few class-specific properties. Mammalian crania are relatively thin and curved, often exhibiting complex shapes that distinguish them from long bone. Cranial fragments display an inner and an outer cortex with some spongy bone in between. This spongy bone (**diploë** is the technical name of spongy bone of the cranium) often appears as long lines of interior bone instead of compact and dense small circles (figure 4.6), which are more characteristic of the weight-bearing spongy bone of other skeletal elements. Another feature that can help to identify cranial fragments is suture lines. Mammalian crania are made up of several bones that grow together at sutures. If present, sutures are visible as squiggly patterns that run across the bone surface on both the inner and the outer cortex. Think of sutures as seams that bring two bones together, similar to how the seams of your clothes bring two pieces of fabric together. The seams may be tight and not allow for movement, or they may be loose and allow the two pieces to separate if force is applied.

Small fragments of human cranial bones are often confused with those of animal bone. Human cranial fragments tend to be more rounded, internally and externally, when compared to those of other mammals. They also tend to have a clearer "sandwich" of spongy bone between two smooth inner and outer bone surfaces or tables. Fragments of turtle shell (carapace) are most commonly confused with human cranial fragments because of the similar curvature, but carapace fragments are not as smooth, often having lines that mimic the exterior shell pattern, much like a soccer ball.

DISTINGUISHING HUMAN CRANIAL
FRAGMENTS FROM NONHUMAN ONES

- Human—Interior and exterior surfaces are relatively smooth but consistently curved, like a fragment of a ball; in cross-section the bone

Figure 4.6. Examples of mammalian cranial bone from archaeological assemblages. A close-up of the thin layer of spongy bone sandwiched between an inner and outer cortex of (left, under 50× magnification, which shows features not visible to the naked eye). The complex shape of mammalian cranial fragments and the characteristic linear arrangement of spongy tissue (center). The spongy tissue of a thicker cranial fragment includes a cranial suture running through the center (right).

    has a clear "sandwich" of distinct spongy bone between smooth cortex bone.

- Nonhuman—Fragments may be flat or otherwise irregular in shape; the exterior may have lines that form a pattern; in cross-section the bone may or may not have a clear sandwichlike appearance.

    The cranial bones of fish are numerous and exhibit complex shapes. Bird crania are much thinner than mammalian crania and rarely survive in archaeological deposits. When they do, the crania are nearly complete, and the very large eye orbits and small brain case simplify their identification as bird crania (figure 4.7). Reptile crania are usually more robust than amphibian crania and can be useful for identification. Cone-shaped teeth are indicative of a reptile. Turtles and tortoises (Testudines) are reptiles without teeth, but their crania are easily identified by the large muscle attachments behind the eye orbits, which help them to pull their head toward their shell for protection. Reptile and amphibian crania also have much more open space than mammal, bird, or fish crania (see figure 4.7) and might be described as holey. The size, shape, and location of each of these openings tend to be more useful for identification than the bony regions themselves.

    Where archaeological assemblages are concerned, the more robust mandibles and teeth are the most identifiable portions of the mammalian skull. Mandibles are much denser than the facial bones, including the maxillae (plural of maxilla) above them. The shape of a mandible, like the teeth it contains, is very much a result of functional morphology related to the feeding habits and therefore can produce genus- and species-level identification with relative ease. If at least some of the teeth are in place in a mandible, a species-level identification is almost guaranteed.

    Mandibles are paired structures; every mammal has a right and a left man-

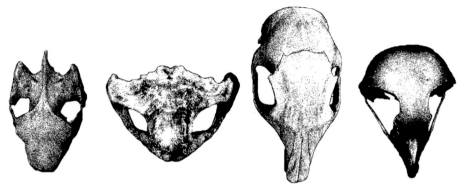

Figure 4.7. From left to right, crania of a reptile *(Clemmys insculpta)*, an amphibian *(Bufo marinus)*, a mammal *(Sciurus carolinensis)*, and a bird *(Otus asio)*.

dible, which are often separated after decomposition or by taphonomic processes. Each half of the mandible, or **hemimandible**, can be sided based on the position of the **symphysis**, the articulation point where the hemimandibles come together. If this portion is missing, you can use the shape of the teeth (right and left side teeth are mirror images of each other) or the position of the **mandibular condyle**, where the mandible articulates with the cranium. Any lateral (side) projections at this condyle usually point medially (inward) for the mandible-to-cranium attachment.

With your mandible sided, compare the shape of the horizontal and vertical **rami** (plural of **ramus**), the horizontal and vertical surfaces of the mandible that join at the back of the mandible. The number and shape of each tooth type that occurs along the horizontal ramus is also very diagnostic. If there is no evidence that the animal had teeth, then you are dealing with a nonmammal, and your mandible is actually a dentary. All modern birds are toothless. Some fish are toothless, while others possess one or more rows of teeth. Reptiles and amphibians may or may not have teeth.

As described in chapter 3, teeth are the most robust and the most identifiable aspect of most animal skeletons. Mammals have a combination of four types of teeth to make up the dentition of one species. These teeth types are the incisors, canines, premolars, and molars. The numbers of each type are called the **dental formula**. Since a mammal can have one dental formula on its mandible and a different dental formula on its maxilla, the dental formula is written as a series of numbers above a line (maxilla formula) and another series of numbers under the line (mandible formula). One of the easiest ways to narrow down the identification of a species from a complete mandible or maxilla is to match the dental formula of your specimen with that of a known species.

DENTAL FORMULAS OF SOME COMMON MAMMALS*

Human—2 1 2 3/2 1 2 3—Mandible and maxilla have the same tooth arrangement.

Cow—0 0 3 3/3 1 3 3—Maxilla has no incisors or canines, but mandible does.

Deer—0 1 3 3/3 1 3 3—Maxilla has no incisors, whereas mandible has six.

Dog—3 1 4 2/3 1 4 3—Mandible has one more molar than maxilla.

*The first four numbers represent the count of the incisors, canines, premolars, and molars in the maxilla. The second set of numbers represents the counts of the same teeth in the mandible.

Teeth that are no longer within the mandible or maxilla can be identified by their overall shape. Incisors are flat in profile and have only one root. Canines are pointed and have only one root. Premolars have a complex crown but only one root. Molars have a complex crown and can have multiple roots. The roots can also differentiate maxillary from mandibular teeth. **Maxillary teeth** have longer and stronger roots than **mandibular teeth**. This makes sense since maxillary teeth need to hang upside down.

As discussed in chapter 3, the dentition of nonmammals is much different from that of mammals. These animals do not have specialized teeth; they do not have the equivalent of incisors, canines, premolars, and molars. Nonmammals tend to have one type of tooth throughout their entire mouth. These teeth are often pointed to serve for both grabbing and tearing of meat. Fish may also have dental plates in their "throats" in addition to or instead of the dentition in the "mouths" (see figure 3.16).

Another important diagnostic element of the cranium is the presence or absence of **antlers** or **horns**. Some ungulates, specifically Artiodactyls, have antlers or horns that grow from their cranium. An important difference between antlers and horns is that horns continue to grow throughout the animal's life, whereas antlers are shed and regrown every season. When the animal is alive, the major difference between horns and antlers is that antlers are covered by soft, velvetlike skin, whereas a hard material, similar to human fingernails and toenails, covers horns. These coverings do not usually survive in archaeological assemblages. Fragments of horns and antlers can resemble fragments of mammalian long bone. Antlers, however, have a much thicker cortex than a long bone, and their interior spongy bones are extremely dense (figure 4.8). The exterior antler cortex has a wood-grainlike appearance that seems exaggerated in comparison to the cortex of mammalian long bone. Fragments of horn are easily identified because the exterior and the interior of horn are more porous than those of antler or long bone. Holes on the exterior surface of horn penetrate the interior in a "Swiss-cheeselike" fashion (figure 4.9).

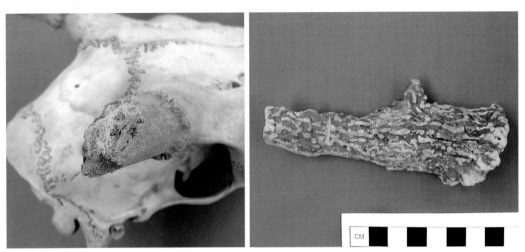

Figure 4.8. Examples of the interior (left) dense sponginess and exterior (right) exaggerated wood-grainlike texture of white-tailed deer *(Odocoileus virginianus)* antler.

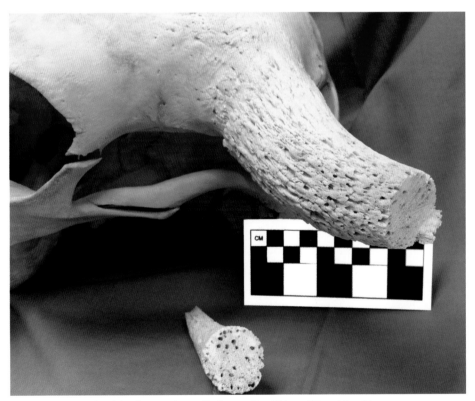

Figure 4.9. Example of the "Swiss-cheeselike" porosity of bison *(Bison bison)* horn.

VERTEBRAE AND RIBS

Vertebrae and ribs are the least diagnostic elements of an animal skeleton because they perform such similar functions in all animals; therefore, their shapes do not vary much from one taxonomic family to another. Vertebrae can be easily identified to the class level because each class has a very different method of locomotion. Most vertebrae and ribs can be identifiable to taxonomic order if they are relatively complete. Genus- and species-level identifications can be difficult. For this reason, vertebrae and ribs are often identified to taxonomic class or order and then assigned to a body size within it (e.g., small mammal or small rodent). See chapter 6 for more about classes of body size.

Vertebrae

To make the class distinctions between vertebrae, a few main differences are useful. Mammals have vertebrae that are quite large relative to their overall body size. This is necessary to support and distribute their body weight for walking and running. Mammalian vertebrae are also complex in shape but always contain a large central hole, or foramen (figure 4.10). The only exception is for caudal (tail) vertebrae. In contrast, fish vertebrae consist of a solid center body, or **centrum**, which is simply round or roundish in shape. From this centrum, one or two long and thin spines are attached. These spines often separate from the centrum in death and may not be part of fish vertebrae recovered from an archaeological site.

The vertebrae of birds are more like those of mammals than of fish; they are complex in shape and contain a central foramen. Bird vertebrae differ from those of mammals in four ways. First, the central foramen is relatively small in comparison to the size of the entire vertebra. Second, most cervical vertebrae of birds contain small, thin, rear-facing projections on the sides (lateral surfaces) of the vertebrae (**hypapophyses**). Third, the articular surface of each vertebra, where the body of one vertebra touches the body of the next vertebra, is essentially flat in mammals but depressed and saddle shaped in birds. This shape allows the bird vertebrae to lock together in order to provide rigidity for flight; the cranial articular surface actually extends outward to fill in the depression that is on the caudal surface. This rigidity is also part of the

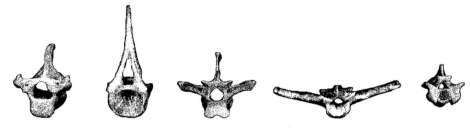

Figure 4.10. From left to right, examples of mammal *(Marmota monax)*, fish *(Stizostedion vitreum)*, bird *(Phasianus colchicus)*, amphibian *(Bufo marinus)*, and reptile *(Python regius)* vertebrae.

fourth difference between bird and mammalian vertebrae, which is that many bird vertebrae are fused to increase body rigidity.

Reptile vertebrae combine traits from all three of the previous classes. The central foramen is present but relatively small with respect to the size of the overall vertebra; the central body is usually round or roundish, and the articular surface is not flat; the caudal surface is depressed, and the cranial surface is extended and ball-like to facilitate the side-to-side motion that occurs when the animal is walking, swimming, or slithering. Turtles and tortoises (Testudines) are again the exception since all but their cervical vertebrae are fused to their shell (carapace), which prevents a side-to-side motion. Testudines also tend to have articular surfaces of their cervical vertebrae, which have two lobes instead of one (see the next text box).

The vertebrae of frogs and toads (Anura) are the most common amphibian vertebrae encountered in archaeological assemblages. Anuran vertebrae tend to have robust lateral projections that resemble the wings of an airplane. The central foramen of all amphibian vertebrae is relatively small when compared to that of mammals. The articular surface of the central body also tends to be relatively flat in comparison to those of birds and reptiles.

CHARACTERISTICS OF VERTEBRAE BY TAXONOMIC CLASS
Mammal—large size with complex shape, large central foramen, flat
    articular surfaces
Fish—roundish solid centrum with little or no central foramen
Bird—complex shape with small central foramen, saddle-shaped
    articulations, rear-facing spines on lateral surfaces, fusion of
    vertebrae
Reptile—small central foramen, roundish central body with a ball-like
    projection at one end and a depressed articular surface at the other
    (turtles have two lobes on central body)
Amphibian—small central foramen, somewhat oval central body with
    relatively flat articular surfaces, large lateral projections

The actual number of each type of vertebrae varies from one taxonomic group to another. This is not of great concern to a faunal analyst since vertebrae counts are rarely an important component of identifying or analyzing a faunal assemblage. If numerous vertebrae are recovered, it is likely that other, more diagnostic elements, like the head or limbs, will also be present. It is important to note that snakes (suborder Serpentes) and animals with long tails can have a large number of vertebrae attributable to a single individual. For example, a site that yields fifty snake vertebrae may have part of only one snake (figure 4.11). See chapter 7 for information on how to count the number of individual animals represented in an assemblage.

To make identifications of vertebrae past the level of taxonomic class, note the differences in overall body size, specialized locomotion (such as hopping), and muscularity. These dissimilarities can be relatively subtle and often require the use of a comparative collection to document. Few bone atlases

Figure 4.11. The 172 vertebrae of a single snake *(Boa constrictor),* strung on a wire.

Figure 4.12. Mammalian *(Marmota monax)* vertebrae showing the range of variation in form within a single skeleton. The atlas and axis, two specialized cervical vertebrae, are on the far left. A single example of cervical, thoracic, lumbar, sacral and caudal forms follow in order.

illustrate the vertebrae, and even fewer illustrate ribs. Some exceptions are Schmid's (1972) and Olsen's (1964) illustrations of the first two cervical vertebrae (the **atlas** and the **axis**) and a single thoracic vertebra, all for common mammals.

A single animal skeleton can contain several types of vertebrae. Mammals have cervical, thoracic, lumbar, sacral, and caudal vertebrae. Cervical vertebrae are easily distinguished from other types (figure 4.12). While all mammalian vertebrae have one hole (foramen) for the spinal column to pass through, only cervical vertebrae have one additional foramen (**foramen transversarium**) on each side of the central foramen (**vertebral foramen**). These additional foramina protect arteries. Cervical vertebrae also have a relatively small central body (centrum) that appears as part of a ring structure.

The body of thoracic vertebrae is much larger and sits below an arch (**neural arch**) that is topped with a long process (**spinous process**) that points toward the tail (caudally). Lumbar vertebrae also have a spinous process, but it is much larger than that of cervical vertebrae while being shorter than that of thoracic vertebrae. The defining features of lumbar vertebrae are their very large **centra** (plural of centrum) and long **transverse processes** that extend to the sides (laterally) like airplane wings. Sacral vertebrae can be easily identified, as they fuse to form the sacrum, part of the pelvis. (See the later section titled "Pelvic and Shoulder Girdles" for more about the sacrum.)

The distal end of the sacrum articulates with the first caudal vertebrae. Caudal vertebrae are much smaller than the other vertebrae and vary in shape along their length. The first few caudal vertebrae may resemble the lumbar vertebrae of a smaller mammal, although their transverse processes tend to point upward (toward the spinous process) instead of downward (toward the centrum) as they do in the lumbar region. Additional caudal vertebrae begin to lose the central foramen and surrounding arch and take on an appearance that ranges from star shaped to circular. The bodies of these distal caudal vertebrae are quite long and therefore not easily confused with other elements.

DIFFERENTIATING MAMMALIAN VERTEBRAE

Cervical—small centrum; overall ringlike shape; three foramina

Thoracic—larger centrum; large spinous process

Lumbar—largest centrum; short spinous process; large transverse
processes

Sacral—fuse to form the sacrum

Caudal—small central foramen or no foramen; small transverse
processes; may appear star shaped in cross-section

The first two cervical vertebrae of a mammal (the atlas and the axis) differ greatly in shape from all others (see figure 4.12). As cervical vertebrae, they have three foramina: two foramen transversariums and one vertebral foramen. The first vertebra, the atlas, bears the bulk of the muscles that attach the cranium to the vertebra and therefore exhibits lateral (side) masses of bone. In large mammals with heavy heads, these lateral masses give an overall rectangular shape to the atlas but one that is very specific to each taxonomic group, and can be used for genus- or species-level identification. The second vertebra, the axis, provides the pivot point on which a head can turn. This is accomplished through a single projection of bone from the central body called the **dens** or **odontoid process**. The axis can also be used to identify the genus and species of a specimen.

In fish the cervical vertebrae (figure 4.13) are distinct from thoracic vertebrae in that cervical vertebrae do not have a fused **neural spine** (spinous process). Thoracic vertebrae have this spine, which extends up from the centrum and points toward the tail (caudally). Following the thoracic vertebrae are the precaudal and the caudal vertebrae. Like the lumbar vertebrae of mammals,

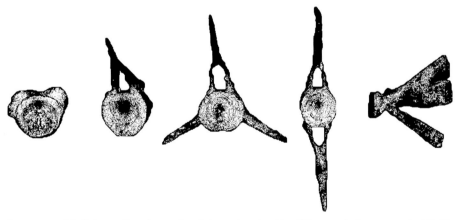

Figure 4.13. Fish *(Stizostedion vitreum)* vertebrae showing the difference between cervical (left), thoracic (second from left), precaudal (center), caudal (second from right), and ultimate (right) forms.

the precaudal vertebrae of fish have transverse processes that extend from the sides of the vertebral body. Caudal fish vertebrae have two fused spines: a neural spine extending upward and a **hemal spine** extending downward. Both spines point caudally. As the caudal vertebrae approach the tail of the fish, these spines become shorter. The last two vertebrae are called the **penultimate** and the **ultimate vertebrae**. The penultimate vertebrae are likely to have only one short spine, and instead of spines, the ultimate vertebra has supports for the tail fin, called the urostyle. The size and the shape of fish vertebrae (and scales) vary along the length of a single fish body in the same way that mammalian vertebrae vary. Each individual fish, however, has many more vertebrae than a mammal, and therefore the degree of variability is significant.

DIFFERENTIATING FISH VERTEBRAE

Cervical—no neural spine

Thoracic—neural spine extends up from central body and points toward tail

Precaudal—neural spine plus transverse processes extending out to sides

Caudal—neural spine plus hemal spine extending downward

Penultimate—only a short neural spine

Ultimate—no spines, support for tail fin present

In birds, the atlas and the axis strongly resemble those of a human, as both support a head that sits atop a vertebral column. Of course, the size of a human vertebra is significantly greater than that of a bird vertebra. As in mammals, the cervical vertebrae of birds contain the three foramen, but the cervical vertebrae of birds also tend to have hypapophyses, small and thin projections of bone that point caudally (figure 4.14), and saddle-shaped vertebral bodies.

A single bird can have up to twenty-five cervical vertebrae (Serjeantson 2009, 22). These are followed by the thoracic vertebrae, which possess a spinous process like that found on mammalian vertebrae. Some or all of these thoracic vertebrae may be fused to form a structure called the **notarium** (see figure 4.14). The lumbar and sacral vertebrae also fuse to form the synsacrum. In adult birds the notarium and the synsacrum may fuse to form a single rigid backbone. Both the notarium and the synsacrum are easily identified by their ladderlike underside, which is formed from the transverse processes of each fused vertebra.

The synsacrum can be distinguished from the notarium by its larger size and the pelvic bones that are fused to its sides. These pelvic bones are much thinner than the fused vertebrae and tend to break off. Some caudal vertebrae are fused to the synsacrum, while others may remain unfused to allow the tail to move. The caudal vertebrae are mainly a central vertebral body with several small transverse and spinous processes. These vertebrae end at a pygostyle,

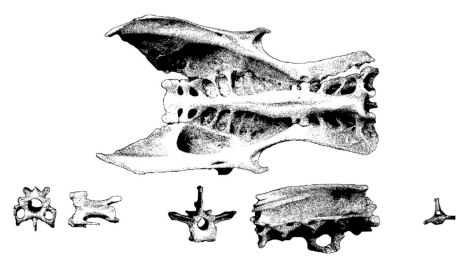

Figure 4.14. Bird *(Phasianus colchicus)* vertebrae showing the difference between a single cervical vertebra (bottom left, end and side view) , a single thoracic vertebra (bottom center, end view), and the fused notarium (bottom center, side view), a single caudal vertebra (bottom, right end view), and the fused synsacrum (top center, anterior view).

which appears as a central vertebral body with a finlike projection that tapers out past the body.

DIFFERENTIATING BIRD VERTEBRAE

Cervical—small centrum; three foramina; rear-facing thin bone projections (hypapophyses)

Thoracic—larger centrum; large neural arch and spinous process; may be fused

Lumbar—fused vertebrae; also fused to sacral vertebrae and pelvis

Sacral—fused to pelvis as part of synsacrum

Caudal—small centrum with spinous and transverse processes

Pygostyle—vertebral body with finlike projection

The vertebrae of reptiles and amphibians do not conform to such simple categories (figure 4.15). Species of these taxonomic classes often challenge our usual definitions of neck, ribcage, back, and tail. There is also much variation from one order to the next. In my experience the most common reptiles and amphibians encountered in archaeological assemblages are turtles and tortoises (Testudines), snakes (suborder Serpentes), and frogs and toads (Anura). Therefore, a quick description of the vertebrae of each follows.

The shell of turtles and tortoises (Testudines) extends from the shoulder girdle to the pelvic girdle. What would be the thoracic and lumbar vertebrae of a turtle are fused to the upper shell, the carapace. The only vertebrae that remain unfused are the cervical and caudal vertebrae. The centrum of a turtle

Figure 4.15. Vertebrae of a turtle (*Terrapene carolina*, left) compared to similar-sized snake vertebrae (*Python regius*, center), showing the range of variation among the reptiles. Note the double-lobed centrum of the turtle and the ball-shaped centrum of the snake. For comparison with a similar-sized amphibian, a toad (*Bufo marinus*, right) vertebra is also shown.

vertebra usually has two lobes, while other reptiles and indeed most animals have only one. This should not be confused with the saddle-shaped centrum of bird vertebrae (see figure 4.14).

Snakes (suborder Serpentes) are made up almost entirely of vertebrae, and one snake can have well over one hundred vertebrae. The cervical vertebrae serve only to attach the head to the rest of the body and are few in number. Most snake vertebrae are **dorsal vertebrae** that articulate with the ribs. A few sacral vertebrae occur toward the end of the skeleton, just before a number of smaller and ribless caudal vertebrae. The dorsal vertebrae are the most identifiable, but the ball-shaped central body of all snake vertebrae, which allows the snake to move in all directions, is distinctive. The ball extends caudally to articulate with the socket in the next vertebra. Because dorsal vertebrae also articulate with the ribs, they have small transverse processes; however, the larger spinous process dwarfs these. Some species also have hemal spines that extend downward (ventrally).

Frogs and toads (Anura) have very few vertebrae, and all except the first vertebra have a distinctive bowtie shape. These vertebrae are dominated by very large transverse processes, like those found on the lumbar vertebrae of mammals. The exact size and shape of these transverse processes are the most useful features for identification.

The large size and unusual shapes of mammalian vertebrae make them prone to breakage. Fragments of vertebrae are commonly recovered from archaeological sites and are easily identified because of their complex shapes (figure 4.16). The centrum or vertebral body of a mammalian vertebra has a somewhat porous surface, with small pores that are visible to the unaided eye. The neural arch (the arch that projects dorsally from the centrum) is a relatively robust portion of mammalian vertebrae, and although it may be separated from the centrum, especially in juveniles, it usually survives intact and is quite identifiable. The ends of the spinous and transverse processes may resemble rib fragments, but they are much thinner than ribs of that size should be, and the spongy bone within them is much thinner.

Fish vertebrae are the only other type of vertebrae that are commonly re-

Figure 4.16. Fragments of mammalian vertebrae from an archaeological site in Maryland. Note the complex shapes of these fragments, which help to identify them as vertebrae.

Figure 4.17.
Fragments of fish
vertebrae from an
archaeological site
in Maryland.

covered as fragments. The bodies of fish vertebrae rarely fragment, but the spines and processes usually break off from the centrum. When this occurs, the centrum resembles a spool of thread, and the spines resemble sewing needles (figure 4.17), the eye of the needle being roughly triangular in shape. The eye is the proximal end of the spine, where it once articulated to the centrum.

Fragments of bird, reptile, and amphibian vertebrae are relatively easy to identify. In birds, fusion of the vertebrae makes them resistant to breakage, and therefore fragments tend to retain enough of the overall vertebral shape to make them recognizable (figure 4.18). In reptiles and amphibians, the small size of the vertebrae makes them resistant to breakage.

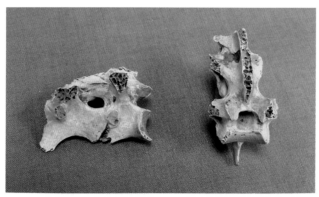

Figure 4.18.
Fragments of bird vertebrae from an archaeological site in Maryland.

CM

IDENTIFYING FRAGMENTS OF VERTEBRAE
- Mammal—tend to break into complex shapes; fragments of centrum are porous; fragments of spinous and transverse processes resemble ribs but are thinner
- Fish—tend to separate into round central bodies and long, thin spines; bodies resemble spools with depressed ends; spines resemble sewing needles with a triangular end at the attachment to the centrum
- Bird—vertebrae are robust and often fused together or to other bones, making breakage difficult
- Reptiles—vertebrae are small and robust, making breakage difficult
- Amphibians—vertebrae are small and robust, making breakage difficult

Ribs

Complete and near-complete ribs are easily recognizable, and a few structural features help to distinguish mammal, fish, and bird ribs. Reptile and amphibian ribs are rarely encountered in archaeological sites, and when they are, more diagnostic elements (such as femurs) should also be present to alert you to their potential presence. Mammalian ribs are usually somewhat square in cross-section. Fish ribs are very long, thin, and curved (figure 4.19). They also are usually transparent to translucent like most fish bone. Bird ribs are much flatter than mammalian ribs, and most contain a process that is unique to bird bone, the **uncinate process**. This process gives bird ribs a forked appearance near the midshaft and serves to increase the rigidity of the chest or thorax.

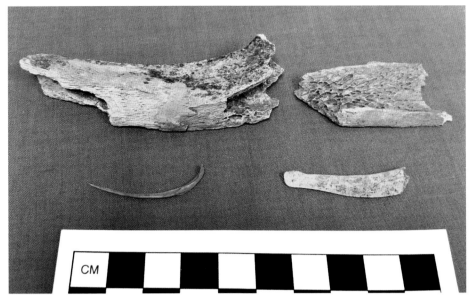

Figure 4.19. Mammal (top row), fish (bottom, left), and bird (bottom right) rib specimens from an archaeological site in Maryland.

Fragments of mammalian ribs are common in archaeological assemblages. Fortunately, it is relatively easy to distinguish rib fragments from those of mammalian long bone. Spongy bone runs along the interior of mammalian ribs and is organized as a series of long, thin bubbles (see fig 4.19). In contrast, the spongy bone that occurs only at the articular ends of mammalian long bone is denser and without a clear pattern of organization.

IDENTIFYING RIB FRAGMENTS
- Mammal—squarish in cross-section; inner spongy bone is more organized and less dense than in long bones
- Fish—very long, thin, and curved with transparent to translucent character
- Bird—flat; some are forked near midshaft for the uncinate process

In mammals, birds, amphibians, and some reptiles the ribs come together at a sternum. **Sterna** (plural of sternum) are not commonly recovered from archaeological sites because they do not always fully **ossify** (become bone) and instead retain the characteristics of cartilage, including easy decomposition. Bird sterna are an important exception because they not only ossify but also are very large bones within the skeleton (figure 4.20). The sternum is where the wing muscles attach to the body. This three-sided bone has very thin walls with somewhat more robust borders and is shaped like an upside-down T

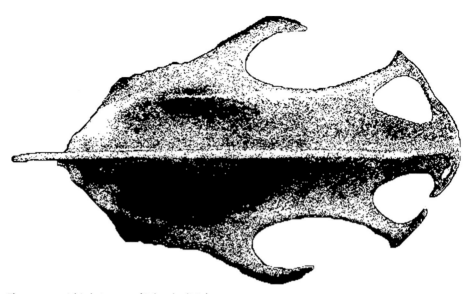

Figure 4.20. A bird sternum *(Columba livia)*.

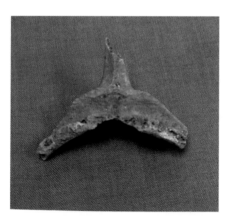

Figure 4.21. A fragment of a bird sternum from an archaeological site in Maryland.

(figure 4.21). If any portion of a bird sternum is recovered, it may be identifiable to the genus or species level with the aid of a comparative collection.

PELVIC AND SHOULDER GIRDLES

The pelvic and shoulder girdles connect the appendicular skeleton (upper and lower) limbs to the axial skeleton. The pelvic girdle usually bears more weight than the shoulder girdle. As a result, the pelvic bones are denser (therefore more commonly recovered from archaeological sites) and more complex in

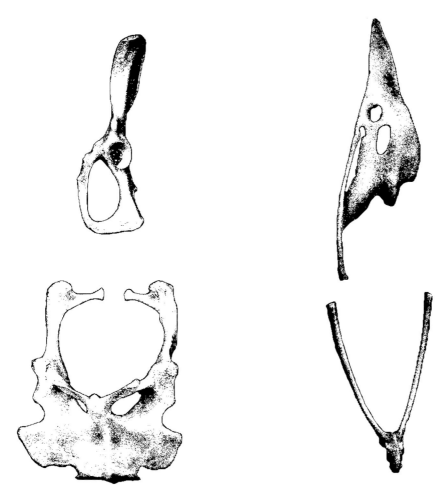

Figure 4.22. The pelves of a mammal (*Sciurus carolinensis,* top left), bird (*Phasianus colchicus,* top right), reptile (*Terrapene carolina,* bottom left), and an amphibian (*Phyllomedusa sauvagii,* bottom right). The mammalian and bird bones shown are side views of one half of the pelvis. The reptile and amphibian bones shown are front views of the full pelvis.

shape (therefore more diagnostic to genus and species) than shoulder bones. The individual bones of both girdles are easily identified to the level of taxonomic class because of their role in animal locomotion.

Pelvic Girdle

Pelves (plural of pelvis) are complex structures made up of several fused bones (figure 4.22). In mammals, the ilium, ischium, and pubis fuse to form an innominate, or os coxa. Each mammalian animal has two innominates, or os coxae, one for each side of the hips. These innominates come together posteriorly (toward the back) at the sacrum and anteriorly (toward the front) at the **pubic symphysis**, the place where the two pubis bones (pubes) meet. Mammalian pelves recovered from archaeological sites often consist of two separate innominates instead of one fused pelvic girdle.

The mammalian innominate is very diagnostic and should allow for genus- and species-level identification if a suitable comparative collection is used. Few bone atlases illustrate the innominate, partially because of the complex shape of this structure. Innominates also have some quite fragile portions, specifically the pubis and the **crest** of the ilium (top of the hip), which are often broken off. Fortunately, the densest region of the innominate, the **acetabulum**, is also the most diagnostic. The acetabulum is the point at which the innominate articulates with the proximal femur.

The exact shape of the acetabulum varies from one species to another because the size and weight of the body of a species, along with its manner and speed of locomotion, dictate the shape. The Schmid (1972) atlas and the Olsen (1964) mammal atlas both illustrate the **acetabular** (of the acetabulum) region for genus- and species-level identification of common mammals. The acetabulum also allows for easy siding of any innominate. The smooth interior articular surface is always in the shape of an incomplete circle (figure 4.23), the break in which points anteriorly and caudally (forward and toward the tail).

Once an innominate is sided, you can also use the break in the acetabulum's articular surface to identify its taxonomic order. Picture the articular surface as the face of a clock. For example, if the space between each lobe of the break would encompass more than ten minutes on your clock face, it is likely the acetabulum of a carnivore, perissodactyl, or primate. Artiodactyls usually have a very small break, accounting for less than five minutes. Rodents vary in the size of their acetabular break, but the acetabulum is not the best diagnostic element of their pelves.

Fragments of mammalian innominates contain a significant amount of spongy bone inside a relatively narrow cortex (figure 4.24). The cortex is also relatively complex in shape but usually contains at least one flat surface. Fragments of innominates are more easily confused with those vertebrae than with ribs. The spongy bone of ribs is more organized than in innominates, and the cortex of innominates is thinner and more complex in shape than it is in ribs. The cortex of vertebrae is usually much more porous than the cortex of pelvic bone and has holes that extend into the interior.

Mammalian **sacra** (plural of sacrum) are not often identified in archaeological assemblages. Although the more proximal portions of the sacrum are relatively dense, the distal portions are not. Fragments of sacrum would resemble fragments of lumbar vertebrae. Few bone atlases illustrate mammalian sacra, so a comparative collection is important to identify sacra past taxonomic order.

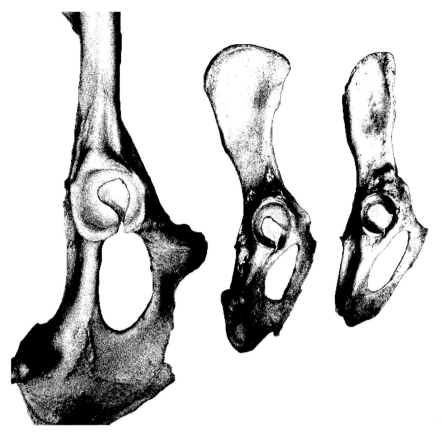

Figure 4.23. The innominates of three mammals, showing the differences at the hip joint (acetabulum). The innominates are from a goat (*Capra hircus,* left), a coyote (*Canis latrans,* center), and a bobcat (*Lynx rufus,* right).

Figure 4.24. Fragments of mammalian pelvic bone from an archaeological site in Maryland.

Figure 4.25. Fragments of bird pelvis from an archaeological site in Maryland. The specimen on the left is a synsacrum; that on the right includes the acetabulum.

Fish have a primitive pelvis that is often located close to the cranium. But since the pelvis is small and fragile and not fused to any other bones, it is rarely recovered in archaeological assemblages.

In birds, the ilium, ischium, and pubis are fused to the synsacrum, the structure that also includes many vertebrae. The pubis extends from this fused mass as a long, thin projection and is often broken off of archaeological specimens. When viewed laterally, the synsacrum should display up to three foramina: the **sciatic foramen**, the **obturator foramen**, and the acetabulum (see figure 4.22). The presence or absence and arrangement of these foramina can be very diagnostic. For example, Galliformes (e.g., pheasants, chickens) have three relatively small foramina. The acetabulum is the most cranially oriented foramen and is surrounded by articular surfaces that form a cup for the femur. One aspect of this cup extends outward from the acetabulum and toward the sciatic foramen; this is called the **antitrochanter**, and its shape and size are also diagnostic. The most recognizable fragments of a bird pelvis are the central section of the synsacrum or the area around the actebular foramen (figure 4.25). These areas are the densest of the bird pelvis.

Like mammals, the pelves of reptiles consist of an ilium, an ischium, and a pubis that meet at the acetabulum. The shape of each of these elements varies greatly among the reptiles, but one general characteristic they all share is a very shallow acetabulum. Some reptiles possess an obturator foramen, a large foramen between the ischium and the pubis. Mammals and birds have this, too. Reptiles with an obturator foramen generally have a deeper acetabulum. Turtle and tortoise (Testudines) pelves are identifiable by their very large pubis, which frames the large obturator foramen (see figure 4.22). When both innominates are together and rotated a certain way, the Testudines pelvis often resembles a party mask worn over the eyes, like those common at Mardi Gras. Some snakes (suborder Serpentes) have primitive pelves, but these are rarely encountered archaeologically and are not very diagnostic.

Amphibian pelves are quite distinct, especially those of frogs and toads (Anura). The acetabulum forms the most robust part of these pelves, especially since the left and right **acetabula** (plural of acetabulum) are fused to form one dense, double-sided articular surface. This surface appears as a large semicircle with a smaller semicircle on each side, resembling a pulley. Extending cranially (upward) from this acetabular body is a long, thin ilium. These **ilia** (plural of ilium) of toads (family Bufonidae) are often broken off in archaeological assemblages (see figure 3.20) but are usually still attached in frogs (family Ranidae). Frog ilia have a **crest**, or ridge of bone, which runs along the ilium down to the acetabulum, enhancing its strength.

IDENTIFYING FRAGMENTS OF PELVIC GIRDLE
- Mammal—complex shape with thin to thick outer cortex and disorganized spongy bone throughout the interior
- Bird—fragments that break off tend to be very thin; otherwise, the fusion makes the bone resistant to breakage
- Reptile—density of the acetabulum and ilium makes these the most common fragments that are still identifiable
- Amphibian—density of the acetabulum and the ilium makes these the most common fragments that are still identifiable

CHARACTERISTICS OF PELVES BY TAXONOMIC CLASS
Mammal—deep acetabulum and large obturator foramen
Fish—located near cranium; has fin-support structures; shaped like a wishbone
Bird—fused to form synsacrum; three foramina form diagnostic pattern
Reptile—very shallow acetabulum, except those with large obturator foramina; turtle and tortoise pelves resemble a party mask
Amphibian—ilium tends to be the most prominent component of the pelvis

Shoulder Girdle

While the pelvic girdle serves to attach the lower limb to the axial skeleton, a similar structure, the shoulder girdle, attaches the upper limb. This structure consists of the scapula (shoulder blade), clavicle, and coracoid (figure 4.26). In mammals, the coracoid is part of the scapula, known as the **coracoid process**. Unlike the pelvic girdle, the parts of the shoulder girdle tend to remain sepa-

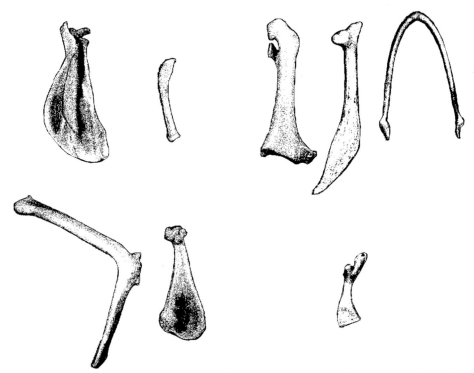

Figure 4.26. The shoulder girdles of a mammal (*Sciurus carolinensis,* top left, scapula and clavicle), bird (*Phasianus* colchicus, top right, coracoid, scapula, and furcula), reptile (*Terrapene carolina,* bottom left, scapula and coracoid), and amphibian (*Phyllomedusa sauvagii,* bottom right, scapula).

rate bones. The scapula and the coracoid are the most diagnostic elements of the shoulder girdle and the most likely to be illustrated in a bone atlas.

Mammalian **scapulae** (plural of scapula) are very distinctive in their overall triangular shape. Most are shaped like an isosceles triangle with the **glenoid fossa**, the equivalent of the acetabulum of the pelvis, located at the apex of the triangle. The bulk of the triangle is thin and flat bone, the **blade**, with little to no interior space for spongy tissue. A crest runs from the glenoid fossa down the blade to the base of the triangle. The most robust parts of the scapula are this crest and the glenoid fossa (figure 4.27). Fortunately, the exact shape of the glenoid fossa is, like the acetabulum, highly diagnostic and can be used to determine genus and species if complete. Ungulates have limited range of motion of their upper limbs, so in general they have fairly simple and shallow glenoid fossae. To facilitate the additional range of motion, nonungulates have two processes, **acromion** and coracoid, which extend from the ridge of the fossa.

Mammalian clavicles are not commonly recovered from archaeological sites

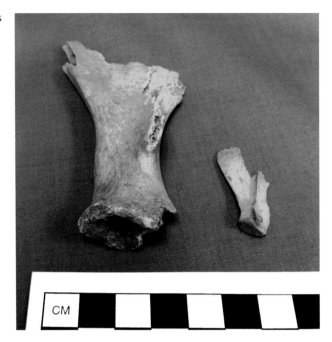

Figure 4.27. Fragments of mammalian scapulae from an archaeological site in Maryland.

for two reasons. First, many mammals do not have clavicles; they are present in animals that have **prehensile** (grasping) hands, like primates and squirrels, and in bats (Chiroptera). Squirrel and bat clavicles are too small to be recovered from most archaeological sites.

Fish do not have scapulas, but they do have clavicles and coracoids. The clavicle is usually fused to the **supraclavicle**, **postclavicle**, **hypercoracoid**, **hypocoracoid**, and the **pectoral rays**, which sit just behind the cranial bones. This shoulder girdle resembles cranial bones with their complex shape and is usually considered part of the head during butchering. However, this complex of clavicle and coracoid bone is generally denser and therefore less translucent than cranial elements.

Bird scapulae do not resemble those of mammals. Instead, they look more riblike, as they are long and thin with a somewhat forked proximal end, where the acromion is located. However, the scapula should not be confused with a rib, as it does not have an uncinate process at the midshaft. The bird coracoid is more distinctive and is usually well represented in archaeological assemblages (figure 4.28) because of its greater density. Many bird coracoids exhibit a hook-shaped proximal articulation that is connected to a fanlike blade by a long, thin neck. The shapes of both the hook and the fan are quite diagnostic. Some species also have distinctive depressions or ridges on the neck or blade that serve to make genus- and species-level identifications. Bird clavicles are usually fused to form the furcula, commonly known as the wishbone. These

Figure 4.28. Fragments of bird coracoid (left) and scapula (right, proximal at top and distal at bottom) from an archaeological site in Maryland.

structures are relatively thin and easily broken and therefore are not well represented in archaeological assemblages.

In reptiles and amphibians, the shoulder girdle often resembles the pelvic girdle but is thinner (less dense) and less diagnostic. The clavicle, coracoid, and scapula come together at a shallow depression for articulation with the humerus. This depression is termed the **glenoid cavity**. In some but not all cases, the pelvic girdle can be distinguished from the shoulder girdle by the flat, broad bones that make up the pelvis instead of the long, thin bones that make up the shoulder. In the Testudines (turtles and tortoises), the shoulder girdles have a scapula that is L-shaped bone with the glenoid fossa where the two arms of the L come together. The coracoid is paddle shaped with a small portion of the glenoid cavity at the thinnest end.

The shoulder girdle of frogs and toads (Anura) comprises a scapula, a **suprascapula**, a coracoid, and a clavicle. The suprascapula is essentially an extension of the scapula blade. In archaeological assemblages the suprascapula is usually detached from the scapula, leaving a roughly triangular scapula with part of a glenoid fossa on one end and an unfinished edge on the other, where the suprascapula should be. The coracoid and clavicle are small and not very diagnostic. The scapula, therefore, is often the most diagnostic element of the Anura shoulder girdle.

CHARACTERISTICS OF SHOULDER GIRDLES BY TAXONOMIC CLASS
Mammal—triangular scapulae; no coracoids
Fish—no scapulae; however, coracoids and clavicles are present as a
    complex of fused bones just behind the cranium

Bird—scapulae are riblike in appearance; coracoids are hooked at one end; clavicles are fused to form furcula

Reptile—shoulder girdle resembles pelvic girdle but with longer and thinner elements

Amphibian—shoulder girdle resembles pelvic girdle but with longer and thinner elements

UPPER LIMBS

Complete limb bones are fairly easy to identify with the aid of a bone atlas; they always illustrate the major limb bones. Because of their complex shapes and the sheer number of bones that would require illustration, the **metapodials**— the bones of the wrists, ankles, hands, and feet—are typically not depicted. Unfortunately, archaeological assemblages tend to contain both metapodials and small fragments of limb bones, not complete ones. Comparative collections of real bone are important for identifying limb bones to the genus and species levels, but some general patterns in morphology help to narrow the search.

The upper limb of a mammal consists of the humerus, ulna, radius, carpals, metacarpals, and phalanges. The same basic plan is found in birds, reptiles, and amphibians (figure 4.29), although some bones have fused and therefore have different names. In amphibians, the radius and ulna may be fused into a radio-ulna. In birds, the carpals and metacarpals have fused to form the carpometacarpus. Despite the variety of names, some universals help to identify the bones of the upper limbs. For example, the proximal articulation on the humerus is always **convex** (rounded or D shaped), that of the ulna or radio-ulna is always **concave** (cupped or C shaped), and that of the radius is usually relatively flat in **profile** (looked at from the side) but relatively circular in **plan** (looked at from above).

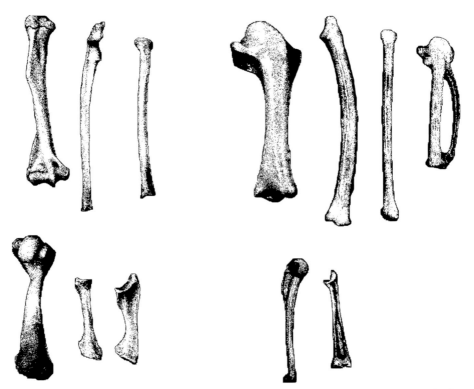

Figure 4.29. The upper limbs of a mammal (*Sciurus carolinensis,* top left, humerus, ulna, radius), bird (*Phasianus colchicus,* top right, humerus, radius, ulna, and carpometacarpus), reptile (*Terrapene carolina,* bottom left, humerus, radius, and ulna), and amphibian (*Phyllomedusa sauvagii,* bottom right, humerus and radio-ulna).

IDENTIFYING UPPER LIMB ELEMENTS
- Humerus—convex (rounded) proximal articulation to form shoulder
- Ulna and Radio-Ulna—concave (cupped) proximal articulation to form elbow
- Radius—proximal articulation is relatively flat in profile but comparatively circular in plan

The mammalian humerus has a proximal head that articulates with the scapula's glenoid fossa. The **head** is a rounded area, slightly larger than the shaft. Adjacent to the head is a round bony projection, or **tubercle**. The size and shape of this tubercle are quite diagnostic (figure 4.30). For example, the largest are associated with the ungulates, such as horses (*Equus* sp.), cows (*Bos* sp.), and pigs (*Sus* sp.).

The proximal humerus connects to the shaft of the humerus without significant constriction (narrowing) below the humeral head. The head is the rounded articulation that sits atop the shaft. This characteristic helps to dif-

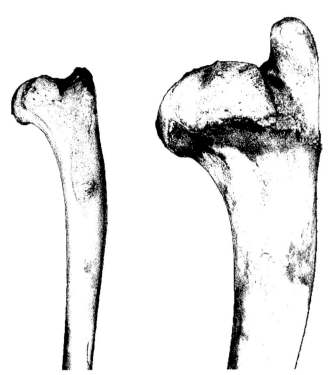

Figure 4.30. Proximal (upper) end of coyote *(Canis latrans)* humerus (left) compared with that of a white-tailed deer *(Odocoileus virginianus)* humerus, showing a much larger tubercle in the deer. This is just one example of the subtle differences in shape that distinguish the long bones of the mammalian species.

ferentiate the humerus from the femur. The shaft of the humerus serves as a muscle attachment area, and therefore one or more crests or **tuberosities** (rounded projections of bone) may occur here. In cross-section the shaft of a humerus is never perfectly round; instead, it appears somewhat twisted (figure 4.31). This twisting usually begins at the midshaft and continues distally until the shaft essentially splits into two segments at the distal articular surface. A depression or a true foramen splits the shaft at the articulation with the ulna.

The degree of twisting varies by genus and species and may be accentuated by ridges of bone that extend down the medial (inner) and lateral (outer) sides of the distal humerus. These ridges allow for greater movement of the forearm and are common in mammals that use their "hands," as humans do. Fragments of the distal shaft, where it splits into two smaller shafts, can be identified by the internal architecture, which is required to support this split. Flush with the interior wall of the shaft are several horizontal reinforcements that resemble a ladder that has melted onto the shaft wall. This architecture is not found elsewhere on the skeleton.

The proximal ulna "hooks in" to the distal humerus. This hook shape is

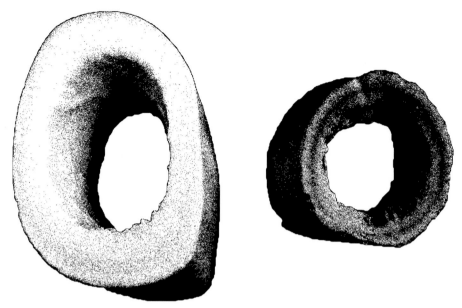

Figure 4.31. Cross-sections of a mammalian humerus (left) and a mammalian femur (right), showing the much more circular shaft, which is characteristic of a mammalian femur.

unique to the ulna and therefore allows for easy identification (figure 4.32). The ulna comprises the **olecranon process** (top of the hook), the **trochlear notch** (the cup of the hook), and the **coronoid process** (the bottom of the hook). In some species the olecranon process is quite small; in others it extends up from the trochlear notch for several centimeters. The shape of the articular surface within the hook is also diagnostic.

The shaft of the ulna varies greatly from one species to the next. In all species it tapers down to a small and simple distal end. In some species the mid-shaft is actually fused to the radius (figure 4.33). In others, such as the horse (*Equus* sp.), the ulna simply ends at its mid-shaft. Fragments of ulna midshaft tend to be small, dense, and somewhat triangulated in cross-section and lack interior spongy bone. The internal cavity is very small, if present at all. These characteristics make this bone one of the most commonly selected for the manufacture of bone tools (see chapter 5), especially bone awls.

The radius is less distinctive in shape than the ulna, except for the fact that both ends of the radius shaft are much flatter than those of other limb bones. It is D shaped in cross-section, with a smooth and curved anterior surface and a flat posterior with one or more raised lines. The distal articulation has multiple depressions (figure 4.34) for articulation with the carpals. The proximal articulation usually has a slight depression for its articulation with the humerus and is generally round to oval in shape. The shape of these articulations allows for genus- and species-level identification. For example, in species with prehensile "hands," the distal articulation includes a small projection known

Figure 4.32. Fragment of a mammalian ulna from an archaeological site in Maryland.

Figure 4.33. The fused ulna and radius of a juvenile white-tailed deer *(Odocoileus virginianus)* showing the unfused distal epiphysis (left) and the large olecranon process extending outward from the proximal articulation (right).

as the **styloid process**. In these species the proximal articulation is also quite simple and relatively round to allow for greater rotation of the forearm. In contrast, ungulates have relatively complex proximal and distal articulations to support limbs that are rigidly locked in place for many hours of standing.

Because of the popularity of chicken wings as food, the upper limbs of birds are relatively easy to identify. Chicken wings usually consist only of the humerus, radius, and ulna. The carpometacarpus and the phalanges are often removed before serving since they contain little meat. The humerus is also often

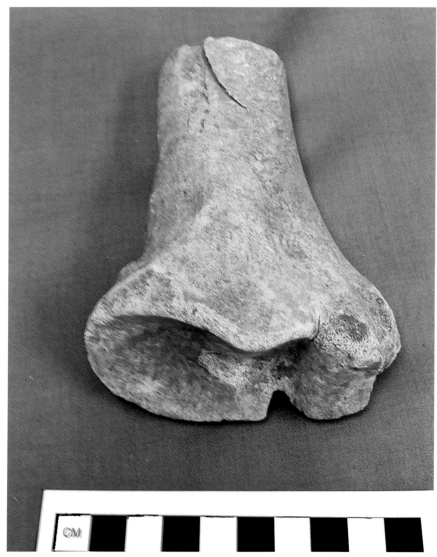

Figure 4.34. Fragment of a mammalian radius from an archaeological site in Maryland.

IDENTIFYING UPPER LIMB FRAGMENTS OF MAMMALS
- Humerus—shaft is a twisted cylinder; proximal end is a round knob; distal end is complex, with the shaft dividing into two parts just before the articulation
- Ulna—proximal end is a hook; shaft is relatively thin but is almost entirely hard cortex; distal end tapers to a point
- Radius—proximal end is flat with a slight depression and round to oval in shape; shaft is often D shaped in cross-section; distal end flares out

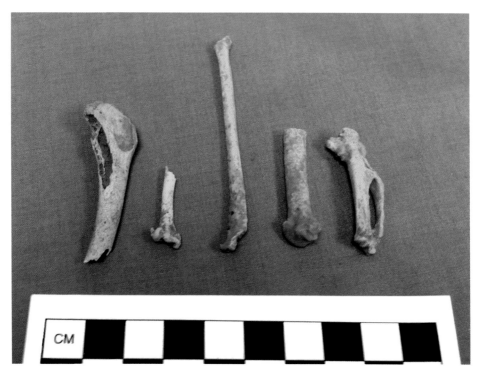

Figure 4.35. Fragments of the upper limbs of a bird from an archaeological site in Maryland. From left to right are a proximal humerus, a distal humerus, a radius, a distal ulna, and a carpometacarpus.

separated from the radius and the ulna, which remain together, as the bulk of their meat lies between the two bones. That allows restaurants to count each wing as two and essentially double-charge you if you are paying by the "wing."

The bird humerus is somewhat similar to the mammalian humerus in that the proximal articulation consists mostly of a protruding rounded surface and the distal articulation is much more complex. Both articulations are useful for identifying a bird humerus to the genus and species level. The proximal articulation usually contains a characteristic depression, or **fossa** (figure 4.35), and a crest opposite it. The size, shape, and placement of these features are diagnostic. For example, Galliformes (e.g., chickens, pheasants) tend to have a defined fossa and a minimal crest. The distal articulation resembles a loosely clenched fist. The size and angle of each of the "fingers" of this fist, as well as the presence or absence of a pointed process just above the distal articulation, can aid in identification. This process is absent in Galliformes but present in most **Charadriiformes** (shorebirds). The shaft of a bird humerus ranges from round to D shaped and is often bowed.

The bird radius and ulna are both long, thin bones with a shaft that is relatively round in cross-section. The ulna is easily identified by the presence of a column of bumps that appears along the shaft in many species. The size and number of these **quill knobs** vary with species. The proximal and distal articulations are less diagnostic, as they are very simple. The proximal articulation is angled down like a ski slope, and the distal articulation has a W shape. Unfortunately, the proximal ulna can resemble the distal radius, although the ulna usually has a more prominent slope. The proximal radius is more distinctive. It is usually roundish with a small, flat depression, or **articular facet**, just below the proximal end. A comparative collection is usually required to discern the subtle differences of these bones from one species to the next. These bones are not often illustrated in bone atlases, and even when they are, the illustrations are not very useful.

The carpometacarpus is unique to birds. This bone is essentially a fusion of the carpals and metacarpals (which form the wrist and palm in humans), and this fusion creates a very dense bone that is well preserved in archaeological assemblages. The proximal articulation is the largest and resembles a pulley. Adjacent to this pulley structure is a small but prominent process; its size and the angle it makes with the pulley are diagnostic to genus and species. Below the proximal carpometacarpus the bone shaft splits completely into two, with one major and one minor shaft. The two rejoin just above the distal articulation. The minor shaft is often broken off in archaeological specimens. Where the two shafts rejoin, the distal articulation is complex in shape with an overhang, or a stepped appearance. The shape of this articulation can also be diagnostic to genus and species.

IDENTIFYING UPPER LIMB FRAGMENTS OF BIRDS
- Humerus—proximal articulation is rounded and contains a diagnostic fossa and/or crest; distal articulation resembles a clenched fist
- Ulna—shaft is relatively round in cross-section; may have a column of raised quill knobs along the shaft; proximal articulation is sloped; distal articulation is W shaped
- Radius—shaft is relatively round in cross-section; proximal articulation is roundish, with a small facet just below it
- Carpometacarpus—very dense and complex-shaped bone; proximal articulation resembles a pulley; shaft is split in two; distal articulation may have a stepped appearance

---

The limb bones of reptiles can be difficult to identify for a few reasons. First, the upper limbs of reptiles are not markedly different from their lower limbs. Second, the shape of the limbs varies greatly from one reptile to the next. Third, both upper and lower reptile limbs are rather shapeless when compared to those of mammals. The overall shape of reptile limb bones can be described as *globular* or *smooth* as one region of bone gradually flows into another. Fourth, very few bone atlases illustrate the limb bones of reptiles. Some illustrations are included in Olsen (1968), Romer (1956), and Sobolik and Steele (1996).

The reptile humerus resembles that of a bird more than that of a mammal. The distal end resembles a clenched fist and is connected to a rounded proximal end by a somewhat bowed shaft. That said, the humerus of a reptile should never be confused with that of a bird, as a reptile humerus is much denser and lacks the fossa on the proximal articulation, which is common among birds. The reptile humerus is somewhat paddle shaped with a woodlike exterior.

Reptile **radii** (plural of radius) and **ulnae** (plural of ulna) are small and lack many clear diagnostic elements. Both tend to be wider at the ends than at the midshaft and are relatively flat in cross-section. Ulnae tend to have some concavity at the proximal end for articulation with the humerus, but some do not. Radii tend to be thinner than ulnae, but both can be long and thin or paddle shaped. The long bones of the Testudines (turtle and tortoise) are somewhat more complex. The proximal articulation of **humeri** (plural of humerus) includes a rounded proximal head with processes on either side of it.

> **IDENTIFYING UPPER LIMB FRAGMENTS OF REPTILES**
> - All are relatively paddle shaped with a dense outer cortex.
> - Articular ends are relatively shapeless when compared to those of mammals.

Amphibian limb bones are difficult to identify to the level of genus and species without an extensive comparative collection, as there are few illustrations in bone atlases because they are difficult to show due to their size and their simplicity. Amphibian limb bones are very long and thin and are therefore relatively easy to identify as amphibian. The articular ends of some are cartilaginous caps, and those in archaeological assemblages often have no ends and may resemble fine tubes.

The humerus of amphibians has an inverted appearance; the rounded articulation is at the distal end. This distal articulation resembles the proximal articulation of a turtle humerus. The proximal humerus usually has a prominent crest on the shaft. Otherwise, the shaft is long and thin with a gentle curvature. The radius and the ulna are usually fused to form a radio-ulna. This bone retains the concavity of ulnae at the proximal articulation. Below this the shaft has a paired appearance, which reflects the fusion of the two bones. The distal end appears as two fused circles.

CHARACTERISTICS OF UPPER LIMBS BY TAXONOMIC CLASS

Mammal—proximal humerus has a rounded knob; proximal ulna has a hook; radius is D shaped in cross-section

Bird—proximal humerus is rounded; distal humerus resembles a clenched fist; radius and ulna are both long and thin; carpometacarpus has a pulley on proximal end and a stepped distal end

Reptile—humerus, radius, and ulna are all globular and somewhat paddle shaped

Amphibian—humerus has a rounded distal articulation; radio-ulna is concave at the proximal articulation and fans out from there with two fused shafts

LOWER LIMBS

The lower limb of a mammal consists of the femur, tibia, fibula, tarsals, metatarsals, and phalanges. The same basic plan is found in birds, reptiles, and amphibians (figure 4.36), although some of these bones have fused and therefore are named differently. In amphibians, the tibia and the fibula may be fused into a tibiofibula. In birds, the tibia, fibula, and some tarsals have fused to form the tibiotarsus, and other tarsals and the metatarsals have fused to form the tarsometatarsus. Some universals help to identify the bones of the lower limbs. For example, the proximal articulation of the femur is always somewhat rounded, and that of the tibia (or tibiotarsus or tibiofibula) is always flat and wide.

The mammalian femur has a distinctive shape (see figure 4.36). The shaft is very long and round in cross-section (see figure 4.31), and the proximal and distal articular ends are much wider than the shaft. Both ends consist of at least two bony projections, but they are never the heart-shaped ends that you see on femurs of the skull-and-crossbones drawings. Like the humerus, the proximal femur contains a round knob of articular surface known as the head. The major difference is that the head of the femur sits atop a narrow segment of bone known as the **neck**, and that neck projects outward from the femur shaft at an angle on the medial (inner) side. (In contrast, the head of the humerus sits directly atop the shaft.) The rounded head of the femur is also recognizable by the presence of a small oval to circular depression near its center, the **fovea capitis**.

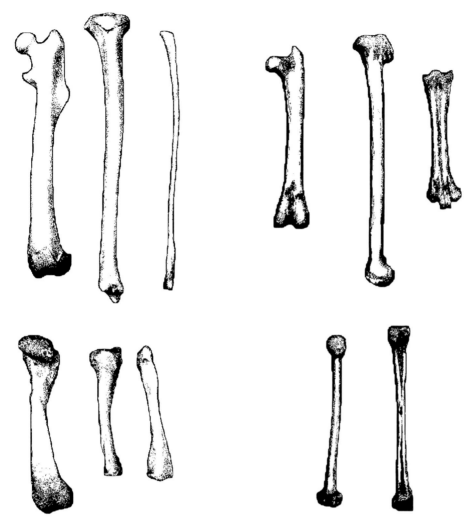

Figure 4.36. The lower limbs of a mammal (*Sciurus carolinensis,* top left, femur, tibia, and fibula), bird (*Phasianus colchicus,* top right, femur, tibiotarsus, and tarsometatarsus), reptile (*Terrapene carolina,* bottom left femur, tibia, and fibula), and amphibian (*Phyllomedusa sauvagii,* bottom right femur and tibiofibula).

The proximal femur can have many other bony projections. On the lateral (outer) side is a muscle-attachment area known as the **greater trochanter**. The greater trochanter does not have any of the smooth articular bone that the head has. Below the **femoral** head, on the medial side, a smaller bony projection can be found, the **lesser trochanter**. The shaft constricts at the base of this second trochanter. Some mammals, such as rodents (Rodentia), have yet another bony projection on the lateral midshaft; this is known as the **third trochanter**. All of these trochanters take the form of ridges or crests, and their exact size and placement can provide genus- and species-level identification. The distal articulation of the femur contains two **condyles** (rounded articular surfaces), one of which is usually larger than the other. The relative size and shape of these condyles have some diagnostic value, but they are not as useful as the proximal articulation in identifying genus and species.

The femur articulates with the tibia. Like the radius of the upper limb, the mammalian tibia is relatively D shaped, as the posterior surface is usually flat. The proximal midshaft takes on a triangular cross-section because of the prominent tibial crest, which projects outward (anteriorly and laterally) and forms part of the proximal articular surface. A fragment of tibia is easily differentiated from a fragment of radius by the location of the raised lines on the posterior surface; those of the radius tend to be more centered on the flat shaft surface, whereas those on the tibia are usually off-center. Fragments of the proximal tibia shaft also often appear as two flat surfaces that have come together at an angle of approximately 60 degrees. This shape does not occur elsewhere on the mammalian skeleton.

Although many bone atlases illustrate mammalian tibiae, these depictions are of limited use if they do not include the view of the proximal and distal articulations from above or below, such as those available in the Schmid (1972) atlas. The proximal end of the tibia consists of two smooth articular surfaces, one for each condyle of the femur; a small ridge that runs from the top of the tibial crest separates these surfaces (figure 4.37). The shape of the proximal articulation is best assessed when looking straight down upon the articular

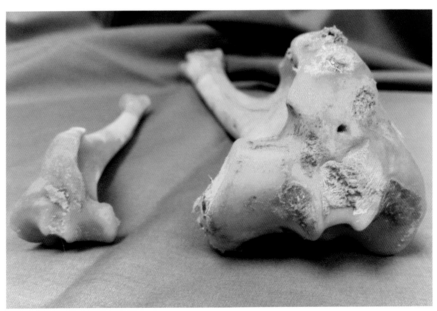

Figure 4.37. Proximal tibias of a coyote (*Canis latrans,* left) and a white-tailed deer (*Odocoileus virginianus,* right) showing the two smooth articular surfaces separated by a central ridge. The tibial crest projects anteriorly (forward or, in this image, upward) from that ridge.

surface. The size and shape of the lateral (outside) articular surface are the most diagnostic features. The distal articulation of the tibia contains a small projection that extends below the distal surface to form the medial (inside) of the ankle (the medial malleolus). To use the distal articulation for genus and species identification, look into the distal articulation to see the two smooth lobes of the articular surface. Make sure the medial malleolus is oriented the same way in each comparative specimen, for the differences here are small. An improperly oriented tibia can easily be misidentified.

The lateral (outside) edge of the tibia articulates with the fibula in most mammals. The distal end of the long, thin fibula pairs with the tibia's medial malleolus as part of the ankle joint, but, like the ulna, it has become reduced or completely lost in many of the ungulates. Horses (*Equus* sp.), cows (*Bos* sp.), and deer (family Cervidae) have only a small bony projection attached to the proximal tibia as all that remains of their fibula. Even when it has not been lost to evolution, the fibula rarely survives in archaeological assemblages. Important exceptions are the Lagomorpha (rabbits, hares) and Rodentia (rodents), in which the fibula is often fused to the tibia. In these cases the point on the tibia shaft where the distal fibula fuses to it can help you to identify genus and species.

IDENTIFYING LOWER LIMB FRAGMENTS OF MAMMALS
- Femur—shaft is very round in cross-section; proximal end has projections known as trochanters; distal end has two large, rounded condyles
- Tibia—proximal shaft is triangular in cross-section; distal shaft is D shaped in cross-section; proximal end has two articular surfaces separated by a small ridge; distal articular end has a medially positioned projection
- Fibula—shaft is long and relatively thin and sometimes is fused to the lateral shaft of the tibia

The lower limbs of birds are easy to recognize. Bird femurs resemble those of mammals in general shape but are always much lighter and thinner than one would expect for a mammalian femur. Despite the general similarity from one bird femur to the next, genus- and species-level identifications are possible. The lateral (outside) condyle of the distal articulation is very useful. All bird femurs have a groove on the posterior (back) surface of this condyle. The groove splits the condyle and creates a shape that is distinctive to the genus. Also useful is the degree to which the lateral condyle projects downward past the medial condyle.

A complete tibiotarsus (see figure 4.36) is easily recognizable by the very

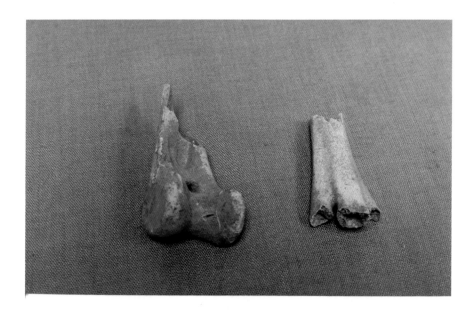

Figure 4.38. Fragments of bird distal tibiotarsus (left) and tarsometatarsus (right) from an archaeological site in Maryland.

angular proximal end, which bears only minimal resemblance to a proximal mammalian tibia. The distal end of a tibiotarsus actually resembles the distal end of a femur, except that the tibiotarsus always has a shallow canal that runs along the posterior (back) surface of the shaft, near the distal end (figure 4.38). Genus- and species-level identifications from the tibiotarsus are more easily obtained from the distal articulation than from the proximal. The shape of the proximal end is quite variable but in an almost abstract way that makes it difficult to describe or illustrate. On the distal end, the location and the depth of a canal and a fossa with respect to the two condyles are specific to genus and species. Fragments of tibiotarsus shaft are identifiable by the presence of a canal on one end and a small crest on the other.

The tarsometatarsus is easily identified by its distinctive three-prong shape, which represents the fusion of multiple metatarsals together. The proximal tarsometatarsus bears some resemblance to a proximal mammalian tibia if the ridges of the tendon canals are mistaken for a tibial crest, but the presence of two foramina, on either side of the ridges, clarifies the identification. Genus and species identifications from the tarsometatarsus are similar to those of the tibiotarsus in that the complexity of the proximal end is difficult to describe and illustrate. The projections of the distal end are much more useful. These pulley-shaped projections are called **trochleas**, and the shape, size, and degree to which one extends below the other two is highly diagnostic. While the center trochlea is usually the most prominent, this is not the case for the **Falconiformes** (e.g., eagles, hawks, falcons) or the Strigiformes (owls). Of those taxonomic groups for which the central trochlea is most prominent, the presence and size of a foramen adjacent to the central trochlea can help to distinguish between two possible groups.

IDENTIFYING LOWER LIMB FRAGMENTS OF BIRDS
- Femur—resembles mammalian femur but has much thinner walls and is lighter in weight
- Tibiotarsus—proximal articulation is very angular; distal shaft has a shallow canal running down it; distal articulation resembles that of a femur but has less prominent condyles
- Tarsometatarsus—distal end has three-pronged shape or three trochleas; proximal articulation resembles that of a mammalian tibia but has two foramina, one on the medial and one on the lateral side of the anterior shaft surface

The lower limbs of reptiles are only slightly different from the upper limbs. In general, the proximal end of a reptile femur bears some resemblance to that of a mammal, but with much less definition. The forked appearance reflects a small femoral head and greater trochanter. The distal end does not resemble that of a mammal or bird femur, for it lacks complexity. The shaft is somewhat bowed. The proximal articulation of turtle and tortoise (Testudines) femurs resembles the proximal humerus of a mammal, with its rounded-knob articulation. Like their radii and ulnae, reptile **tibiae** (plural of tibia) and **fibulae** (plural of fibula) lack many clear diagnostic elements.

IDENTIFYING LOWER LIMB FRAGMENTS OF REPTILES
- All are relatively paddle shaped and have a dense outer cortex.
- Articular ends are relatively shapeless when compared to mammals.

The femurs of amphibians are very simple and often resemble long, thin tubes of bone. Tibiae and fibulae fuse to form a tibiofibula that resembles the long and thin femur, but the end of a tibiofibula is slightly forked—a remnant of the fusion. As such, the bone has an almost X-shaped appearance, where the X is very long, thin, and compact. A small depression or foramen often appears at the center of the X. In archaeological assemblages, amphibian femurs and **tibiofibulae** (plural of tibiofibula) often lack their articular ends and therefore appear as long and thin but slightly curved bones.

IDENTIFYING LOWER LIMB FRAGMENTS OF AMPHIBIANS
- Femur—long and thin with no clear features
- Tibiofibula—resembles a long, thin, and compact X shape with a depression or foramen at the center

CHARACTERISTICS OF LOWER LIMBS BY TAXONOMIC CLASS
Mammal—femur has two large projections at each end; tibia is triangular at proximal end and D shaped at distal end

Bird—femur resembles that of a mammal but has a less distinctive shape; distal end of tibiotarsus can be mistaken for a femur, but the proximal end is very tibia-like; tarsometatarsus has complex three-pronged shape to distal articulation

Reptile—femur, tibia, and fibula are all somewhat paddle shaped

Amphibian—femur and tibiofibula are long and thin with few features

HANDS AND FEET (MANUS AND PES)

Mammals, amphibians, and reptiles have various arrangements of carpals and tarsals that form wrists and ankles. Carpals and tarsals are compact bones (figure 4.39) with smooth articular surfaces on more than one side or face of the bone. For all metapodials (carpals, tarsals, metacarpals, metatarsals, and phalanges), concave articulations are usually located on the proximal surface, and convex articulations are on the distal surface.

Carpals and tarsals pose a problem for faunal analysts because few bone atlases illustrate them. Comparative specimens are often required to identify carpals and tarsals to genus and species, yet few comparative collections have

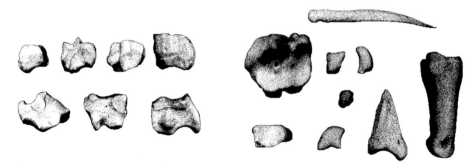

Figure 4.39. Carpal and tarsal bones and some phalanges of a white-tailed deer *(Odocoileus virginianus)* showing the variety in shapes but the common compact nature of these elements.

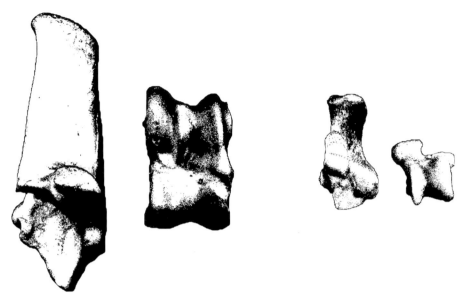

Figure 4.40. Calcaneus and astragalus of a large mammal (*Odocoileus virginianus*, left) compared with that of a small mammal (*Marmota monax*, right).

them labeled with the correct name and side of the body that they are from. Fortunately, the small size of most carpals and tarsals makes them difficult to recover from archaeological sites. When they are recovered, usually other elements of the same animal are also present. Therefore, the best approach to identifying carpals and tarsals is to compare those recovered with specimens from those species already identified within the assemblage. Still, most carpals and tarsals from archaeological assemblages are identified only to taxonomic class and body size (e.g., small mammalian carpal).

Two of the largest tarsals are an exception, the **calcaneus** and the **astragalus** (figure 4.40). These bones articulate with the distal tibia and have the same basic shape in most mammals; the calcaneus has a long, thin end, shaped somewhat like a handle. This forms the animal's heel. The astragalus is a more squarish, compact bone with at least one pulleylike articular surface, which allows the heel to move up and down. In ungulates the astragalus is usually somewhat rectangular but with distinctive rounded edges, giving the bone an almost S-shaped appearance when viewed from the side (figure 4.41). In some other mammals the astragalus has a rounded bony projection that resembles the handle of the calcaneus and can lead to misidentification. The calcaneus can be distinguished from these calcaneus-like **astragali** (plural of astragalus) by its distal end, which has several smooth articular surfaces, and its proximal end, which has no articular surfaces.

Distally, carpals and tarsals articulate with each other or with metacarpals (upper limbs) or metatarsals (lower limbs). Metacarpals or metatarsals are

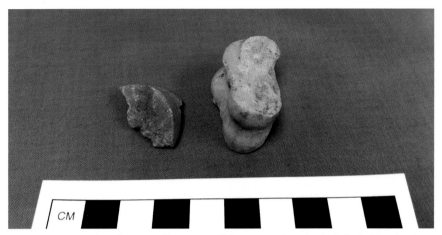

Figure 4.41. Examples of mammalian astragali from an archaeological site in Maryland. The specimen on the left is a fragment from a very large mammal.

the bones that form the palm of a human hand or the ball of a human foot. These are often the most diagnostic elements of the manus and pes. Because of their larger size, these bones are easier to recover from archaeological sites than carpals, tarsals, or phalanges. However, their identification is still problematic, as a wide variety of shapes occurs in animals; similarities can be found among animals with comparable modes of locomotion and range of dexterity. Prehensile hands and feet (those capable of grasping) are quite different from those that are not prehensile. In general, each mammalian metacarpal or metatarsal has articular ends that are wider than the shaft. The bones are quite robust, and in those with fewer metacarpals or metatarsals, evidence of fusion is readily visible (figure 4.42). In all cases the distal end has a pulley-shaped, rounded projection (trochlea) for articulation with the phalanges. In ungulates this distal end is complex and resembles multiple pulley systems.

Metacarpals and metatarsals of the same animal are very similar in appearance; both have a very dense outer cortex with little interior spongy bone. Metacarpals can be distinguished from metatarsals by their smaller size, as they bear less weight. The smaller size is in width rather than length. For example, among ungulates the proximal metacarpal is clearly D shaped, whereas the proximal metatarsal is almost square. In mammals the actual number of metatarsals and metacarpals is specific to genus. Horses (*Equus* sp.) have one large metacarpal and one large metatarsal, each flanked by much smaller metacarpals or metatarsals, one on each side. Cows (*Bos* sp.) have one metacarpal and one metatarsal. Pigs (*Sus* sp.) have two medium-sized metacarpals and metatarsals in the center of their manus and pes and two smaller metacarpals or metatarsals, one on each side of the two central ones.

The hands and feet of mammals, birds, amphibians, and reptiles all end in phalanges that have the same basic shape; a wide proximal end with a concave

Figure 4.42. A complete metatarsal and two fragmentary metacarpals of a white-tailed deer *(Odocoileus virginianus)* showing evidence of fusion in the interior of the fragments as a central ridge and on the exterior by the canal that runs the length of the bone.

articular surface, a somewhat thinner shaft, and a distal end with either an articular surface or a tapered point (see figure 4.39). However, the phalanges within a single animal can display significant variation depending on what digit (finger or toe) it is from and even which segment of that digit it is from (most human fingers are made up of three segments or individual phalanges). Figure 4.39 shows two phalanges from the same animal in the lower right-hand corner. The pointed phalange is a distal (or terminal) phalange, the last one of that digit, while the longer one to its right is a proximal phalange, a phalange between the metacarpal or metatarsal and the distal phalange.

A single animal has two to four phalanges per digit, each with its own distinctive shape. Due to the significant degree of variety, phalanges are not easily identified to genus or species without an adequate comparative collection. The terminal phalanges, those that form the finger pad, hoof, or claw base, are easily identified to taxonomic order. Perissodactyls (e.g., horses) have a short, squat, and arc-shaped terminal phalange. Artiodactyls (e.g., cows, deer, goats) have a triangular terminal phalange. Carnivores (e.g., dogs, bears), rodents, and lagomorphs (rabbits and hares) have a pointed and clawlike terminal phalange.

CHARACTERISTICS OF MAMMALIAN METAPODIALS
Carpals—often resemble small rocks but have many smooth articular
    surfaces in between rough surfaces; usually smaller than tarsals
Tarsals—larger size and more complex shape make them easier to
    identify than carpals
Metacarpals and Metatarsals—distal end has knob shape or pulley shape
Phalanges—proximal end is concave; distal end is convex; a small shaft is
    in between

The carpals and tarsals of birds are part of the larger carpometacarpus and tarsometatarsus that were discussed earlier with regard to limb bones. Carpals and tarsals of reptiles and amphibians are not commonly encountered in archaeological assemblages because of their small size. Exceptions are the calcaneus and astragalus of Anura (frogs and toads). Both are long, thin bones that resemble the radius and ulna of a bird more than the calcaneus and astragalus of a mammal. They are often found attached to each other, but they are not fused in the center; instead, they are completely separate at their midshaft and come together at their ends. The metacarpals and metatarsals of amphibians and reptiles are not very distinctive and tend to resemble phalanges but with a more complex proximal articulation.

SIDING BONE

Once you have identified your specimen to a skeletal element (e.g., femur) and taxonomic group (e.g., *Odocoileus* sp.), it is important to determine which side of the body that specimen came from. This information is crucial for the minimum number of individuals calculation (see chapter 7). Of course, not all bones have sides. Vertebrae and any other bones that come from the center of the body (the axial skeleton) are not sided.

Siding bone is simple if the bone is complete and you have access to a comparative collection where rights and lefts are labeled as such, but this is often not the case. Remember that, unless stated otherwise, bone atlases usually illustrate the left side of all bones that can be sided. These atlases are very useful for siding fragments, not just complete bones, if they have distinctive features or landmarks on them. The exact shape of these landmarks and their position relative to each other will either match the illustration of that bone in your atlas or be the mirror image of it. A match says your specimen is a left. A mirror image says your specimen is a right. Over time you will begin to remember the relative placement of bone landmarks and be able to side without referring to an atlas at all. To reduce the amount of time spent consulting reference material, develop ways to remember general patterns that you observe. For example, any mammalian tibia is most easily sided by the shape of the tibial crest, which points outward laterally, or toward the side the tibia is from.

Many new faunal analysts have trouble siding elements from the upper limbs. Because the arm has more flexibility than the leg, the arm joints are more variable in form than the leg joints. What may be helpful here is to remember that the smoothest surface of a bone tends to be the anterior surface, the one facing outward when the bone is in anatomical position. Also, bones that have curvature to them tend to be convex toward the anterior (front) and lateral (side) surfaces. Flat surfaces of bones tend to be posterior (back) surfaces. These are general rules, however, and they do not work with all bones.

When attempting to side fragments of mammalian long bone, the placement of **nutrient foramina** may be helpful. Nutrient foramina are holes that reach from the outer surface of a long bone into the marrow cavity to transport nutrients. They are always at an angle; they do not go straight into the bone. There is a pattern to the angle; foramina at the proximal end of a long bone point downward (you would have to shine a light down into the foramen to have any hope of seeing inside the marrow cavity), and those at the distal end point upward (shine the light up into the cavity). This pattern should not only help you to properly orient your long bone fragment, but, together with the curvature of the bone around that foramen, may also be all you need to identify a small fragment of mammalian long bone to genus, species, element, and side.

DETERMINING SEX AND AGE

Determining sex and age is not always easy and not always worth the investment of time. Although humans spend many years growing, other animals grow very quickly. **Epiphyseal fusion** (the timing of the fusion of the epiphyses to the shaft) is therefore much more useful for determining the age of humans than of nonhumans. In general, specimens with missing or incompletely fused

Figure 4.43. Examples of unfused epiphyses from an archaeological site in Maryland. The specimen on the left is the epiphysis of a calcaneus; in the center is the distal end of a juvenile tibia; to the right is a fragment of vertebra epiphysis.

epiphyses (figure 4.43) can be considered a juvenile. However, specimens with completely fused epiphyses are not necessarily adults. Most mammalian bones have more than one epiphysis, and each fuses at a different time. Only those specimens that have all their epiphyses completely fused are clearly adult.

Age can also be estimated from mammalian teeth. Patterns of wear can be checked against reference charts for that species, or they can be **thin-sectioned** to look for growth rings. However, wear patterns are dependent on the types of food consumed and the environment in which the animal lived. For example, the teeth of a pig kept in a pen near a grassy field with silty clay soil will wear more slowly than those of a free-range pig in a sandy, desertlike rangeland.

Only the bones of adults show clear indicators that the specimen is from a male or a female. For example, adult males of the taxonomic order Galliformes, including domestic chickens *(Gallus gallus),* often have a prominent spur on their tarsometatarsus. Therefore, if you have a fully developed *Gallus gallus* tarsometatarsus with a spur, you know it likely comes from an adult male. Nonetheless, the presence of a spur does not equate to an adult male; there are some documented cases of **hens** (females) with spurs, and in either case spurs are often removed from domestic birds to prevent them from harming one another.

Antlers are a similar case in point. Adult male deer (e.g., *Odocoileus* sp.) grow antlers each year, which are shed after the mating season. Therefore, the presence of antlers indicates the presence of an adult male deer (buck); however, there are some documented cases of adult female deer (does) with small antlers. Within the same taxonomic family of Cervidae (deer and elk), all adult males grow antlers, but in one species—the caribou or reindeer *(Ran-*

Figure 4.44. The baculum of a raccoon *(Procyon lotor)*.

gifer tarandus)—the females also grow antlers. So the presence of antlers suggests but is not necessarily indicative of an adult male.

Males are not the only sex that have useful but unreliable characteristics. Female birds can be identified by the presence of **medullary bone** within broken long bones. Medullary bone resembles a white or light-colored stuffing and is present in the shafts of long bone before eggs are laid. Since the presence of medullary bone is often season specific, it does not occur in the long bones of all female birds. So medullary bone is not necessarily indicative of an adult female (and breaking a long bone to look for medullary bone is not recommended; see discussion of broken bone in chapter 5).

There are a few additional sex indicators that most faunal analysts know. For example, males of the taxonomic family Suidae (hogs and pigs) tend to have significantly larger canines than the females. Both males and females have tusks, but the males' tusks are much larger and curved. Canines are also smaller in females of some other taxonomic groups, including the family Equidae (horses, asses, and zebras), where they may be absent altogether. Within the taxonomic order Carnivora, the families of **Mustelidae** (badgers, otters, weasels), **Felidae** (cats), and **Procyonidae** (coatis, raccoons) show the most sexual dimorphism (one sex is usually significantly larger than the other).

Sexual dimorphism is a reliable way to determine sex from skeletal remains, but only for those species that exhibit it. Most primates are sexually dimorphic, with males tending to be larger than females of the same species. A series of measurements can be made on certain bones and plugged into a formula to determine the likely sex of the individual from which the specimen came. The exact measurements necessary will depend on the species under consideration. Since this work requires repeated measurements to be made and recorded on a separate spreadsheet, such measurements are best made after the entire assemblage has undergone cataloging. Simply set aside the bones that will undergo this secondary analysis in individually labeled bags for now. If the specimen was removed from a bag that contained other specimens, you may wish to slip a piece of paper into the larger bag that describes what has been removed, by whom, and why. That way if someone is looking for the same specimen, that person will be able to find it if needed.

A popular but uncommon sex indicator is the **baculum**, or penis bone. Males of the taxonomic orders Carnivora (carnivores), Rodentia (rodents), and Primates tend to have a baculum (figure 4.44). Humans, members of the primate order, are an exception. The baculum does not directly articulate with any other bone. Without the aid of a comparative collection, it can be difficult to identify a baculum to the species level, as most bone atlases do not illustrate them, but they are also not commonly found in animal bone assemblages.

5   What Else Can the Bone Tell Me?

Identifying bone and bone fragments to skeletal element and taxonomic group is just the beginning of what you can learn from an archaeological assemblage. Bones also contain a wealth of information about their taphonomy, that is, everything that happened to the animal from the time it died until the time a portion of its skeleton was analyzed in your lab. This information is encoded in **taphonomic signatures**, marks on or discoloration of the bone, and in the presence or absence of specific bones or portions of bones.

Taphonomic analysis of an assemblage is based on patterns. Therefore, it is important to decide what taphonomic information you are going to collect early on. If these data are not compiled for each and every specimen, any resulting patterns may be more a reflection of data collection than of the assemblage itself. Some of the most common taphonomic signatures are discussed in detail in this chapter. Consider building your own comparative collection of examples of different taphonomic signatures. This will help standardize your identification of them.

Most taphonomic signatures are visible with the naked eye, but they should be viewed under 10× or 50× magnification to assess their shape and size. This can be done with a standard loupe (see chapter 2), a standard stereomicroscope, or a digital microscope. For those working in an academic setting, stereomicroscopes can be found in many science classrooms. For those without access to stereomicroscopes, digital microscopes are relatively inexpensive and allow for the easy capture of images.

> **TOOLS OF THE TRADE**
> Stereomicroscope or digital microscope for viewing taphonomic signatures at 50× magnification—available from science supply stores, electronics stores, or science classrooms

BROKEN BONE

Most archaeological assemblages consist mainly of bone fragments. As discussed in chapter 2, some of these fragments were created by excavation of the site and recovery of the bones themselves. The taphonomic signature of these processes is usually freshly broken edges. I advocate mending as many fresh breaks as possible to reduce bias caused by archaeology, inasmuch as this will return the assemblage to a condition more closely representative of the state it was in before excavation began. But there are two other types of broken bones: bones that the people who lived at the site broke intentionally (such as for marrow extraction) and bones that were broken unintentionally by people, animals, or other natural processes. Although it is not possible to determine how and why each and every break has occurred, certain patterns may be recognizable through analysis of bone breaks.

Reconstructing the fragments of a broken bone can be useful in determining whether the break was intentional and whether it is cultural or natural in origin. Bone that has been broken soon after the animal's death usually shows some deformation near the break. The fresh bone is moist, and that moisture causes the bone to deform, much like a live twig would do if pressure were applied to it. Only after the limit of deformation has been reached does breakage occur. For this reason, fresh breaks with deformation of the bone are called **greenstick fractures**. Once an animal dies, its bones dry out and become brittle. Instead of deforming, these dry bones shatter under pressure, resulting in angular or **stepped fractures**.

In many cultures the shafts of long bones are routinely broken to recover the **marrow** within them. Marrow is a calorie-rich fatty substance found in the shaft of long bones. Marrow extraction breaks are usually, but not always, **spiral fractures**, fractures caused by excessive twisting of bone shafts. A spiral fracture is visible as a diagonal break across the shaft of the long bone. In some cultures marrow recovery is more extensive, and other skeletal elements, like the mandible, are also fractured. These other elements may be broken by **indirect** or **direct percussion**, applying a force to break the bone with or without a solid object between the "hammer" and the bone to be broken. Direct percussion may be evident as a **compression fracture**, in which the point of impact appears as an area of crushed bone. Indirect percussion may resemble a **puncture wound** on the bone surface, showing a clear point of impact but little damage to the surrounding bone.

To evaluate the extent of marrow extraction and the methods by which this extraction took place, an analyst may need to temporarily reconstruct skeletal elements. With experience an analyst should be able to recognize different types of breaks (figure 5.1) without the need to reconstruct any fragments.

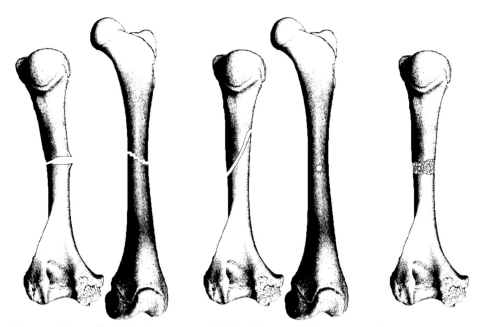

Figure 5.1. Types of bone fractures: greenstick (far left), stepped (second to left), spiral (center), puncture (second to right), and compression (far right). These drawings are intended to exaggerate the differences between the fracture types. Actual bone fractures will not appear so distinct.

CUT BONE

Although most archaeological bone is the result of butchering animals for meat, only a portion of any assemblage will contain clear butchery marks. Unless your assemblage dates from a time when metal saws and large cleavers were used to cut through bone, the people who created your assemblage avoided cutting into bone, as this would unnecessarily dull the edges of their tools. Given the relatively low incidence of butchery marks on archaeological bone, when these marks are encountered, they should be recorded to provide data on how animals were segmented and what cuts of meat were obtained. Not all cut marks are directly related to meat acquisition; some may be the result of skinning an animal for its hide, and others may be the result of cutting larger bodies into smaller segments for transport or sale.

Again, what is important in faunal analysis is an analyst's ability to recognize patterns. The location and form of each and every single cut mark is part of a pattern of animal processing, a cultural practice for which there may be no other evidence. Identify where the bone was cut, and also look for evidence of the type of tool used and the purpose of the cut. For example, surface cut marks, or **knife cuts**, are marks created when a cutting edge is dragged across a bone surface. A true cut mark should be longer than it is wide (figure 5.2) and should taper to a point at its maximum depth, revealing a V shape. This

Figure 5.2. Two examples of cut-marked mammalian bone identified in an archaeological assemblage, viewed with 50× magnification, which shows features not visible to the naked eye.

provides a rough estimation of the cutting implement. The location and orientation or direction of the cut can be used to determine whether the mark was made during dismemberment or meat removal.

Saw marks are more rectangular in cross-section than knife cuts, and they penetrate more deeply into the bone. Saws marks actually contain a lot of information about the type of saw used. To learn how to recognize saw marks, saw a piece of wood and then look at the interior cut surface. You will see a series of lines that are made as the teeth of the saw rake across the surface to cut it. The length and the direction of each of these lines are a record of every stroke made by your saw. Lines that are perfectly straight and parallel to each other are likely those of an electrical band saw; those that are equally spaced but are curved like an arc are likely those of an electrical circular saw. Lines that are neither equally spaced nor parallel are likely those of a handsaw, like a hacksaw. Human-powered cutting is not as uniform as electrically powered cutting.

> **IDENTIFYING CUT MARKS**
> - Knife cut—longer than they are wide; V shaped in cross-section
> - Band saw—straight parallel lines that are equally spaced
> - Circular saw—curved parallel lines that are equally spaced
> - Hacksaw—lines of various orientations and not equally spaced

To reconstruct patterns of butchery, many faunal analysts find it useful to record the location and orientation of all observed cut marks on species-specific skeletal diagrams. Recording all cow-bone cut marks on a drawing of a cow and all pig-bone cut marks on a drawing of a pig provides a summary of butchery patterns for interspecies comparisons. Such diagrams (figure 5.3)

Figure 5.3. Examples of recorded butchery patterns from an archaeological site in New York. The top image identifies the location and direction of all cut marks observed on Canidae specimens. The bottom image does the same for all Cervidae specimens.

are often included in technical reports or published in articles, thus allowing for quick intersite comparisons.

WORKED BONE

There are two different ways to approach **worked bone**, bone that has been used as a raw material, most often for the creation of a tool or an ornament. Some treat worked bone as an artifact, like a piece of pottery, and keep it separate from the faunal assemblage. When this happens, data will be missing from the faunal-based assessment of how the site inhabitants used animals. However, when the worked bone is not separated from the faunal assemblage, the artifact may never be identified, and therefore data will be missing from the artifact-based assessment of the activities that took place at the site. The best approach is to catalog all worked bone with unworked bone but to keep it separate from the rest of the faunal assemblage so that an artifact expert can also analyze it.

Worked bone is often easy to recognize, as the bone or bone fragment has been modified to take on a specific shape. For example, the awl is a common form of bone tool. Awls are often created from the shafts of a mammal ulnae, metatarsals, or metacarpals, although they can be made from almost any bone. Awls have a characteristic pointed tip at one end (figure 5.4), which was commonly used for puncturing hides in the manufacture of clothing.

Unfortunately, a standard means for analyzing worked bone does not yet exist, although there are some good examples of the type of analysis that is possible. One such example is that of the Arroyo Hondo Pueblo project (Beach and Causey 1984). Arroyo Hondo is an archaeological site in New Mexico. The analysis of animal bones from this site included the creation of a typology of bone tools, ornaments, musical instruments, stone-knapping tools, and hide-

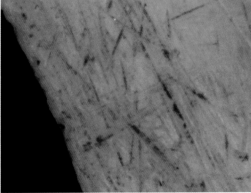

Figure 5.4. Two examples of worked mammalian bone identified in an archaeological assemblage, viewed with 50× magnification, which shows features not visible to the naked eye. The image to the left is of an awl with a broken tip.

processing implements that can be adopted when analyzing similar assemblages from the American Southwest.

Of course, before one can classify worked bone to a specific typology, one has to be able to recognize worked bone with some level of certainty. Worked bone tends to have a polished look; in the case of tools, this is often a result of oils from the user's hands. Under 10× or 50× magnification the working appears more organized (see figure 5.4) than would be possible from a natural source, like unintentional trampling of bone by humans or animals. **Trampling marks** are created when bone rubs against grit (like sand) and are recognizable as disorganized lines that are often not straight.

IDENTIFYING WORKED BONE
- May appear polished from the oils of human hands holding it or from the material the bone tool (such as an awl) was used on.
- Under magnification, the abrasion marks left by the shaping process appear somewhat organized.

BURNED BONE

Burning changes bone color and hardness, but the exact outcome depends on several factors, including the moisture content of the bone and the temperature and duration of heat exposure. The two main categories of burned bone are **charred bone**, which appears black or blue, and calcined bone, which appears gray or white. A single bone can show varying degrees of charring and calcification depending on the conditions of its burning (table 5.1).

Complete calcination of a bone requires extended exposure to high heat and the absence of moisture during this exposure. Calcination is most commonly associated with relatively clean bones that have been disposed of in a fire for routine trash disposal or for ritualistic cremation. Calcined bone is very brittle and is easily broken into angular fragments whose internal surfaces are also

Table 5.1. The impacts of fire temperature on bone color in bone burned under certain experimental conditions (Adapted from Gilchrist and Mytum 1986)

Temperature (Celsius)	Color Description
200	very pale brown
300	brown to dark reddish brown
350	dark brown to black
420	bluish gray
500	light gray
600	pinkish gray
700	white

white. If the bone has not become completely calcined, a break will reveal a black interior. Calcined mammal bone should produce a fine powder when scratched across the surface with a fingernail. This can help distinguish calcined bone from bone that has been weathered white, or sun-bleached (see the following section, "Weathered Bone").

> **IDENTIFYING CALCINED BONE**
> - Calcined bone can usually be scratched with a fingernail, producing a fine powder on the nail.
> - Incompletely calcined bone may have some black bone in the interior.

Often only a portion of a bone is charred. This most commonly occurs during roasting, where meat was present on a portion of the bone, protecting it from direct heat (figure 5.5). In these cases careful documentation of the pattern of bone charring can provide valuable information on cooking methods used. Alternatively, partial burning of a bone can prepare it for working or for a specific tool function by increasing its hardness. In these cases careful documentation of bone charring can provide helpful information on artifact manufacture or use.

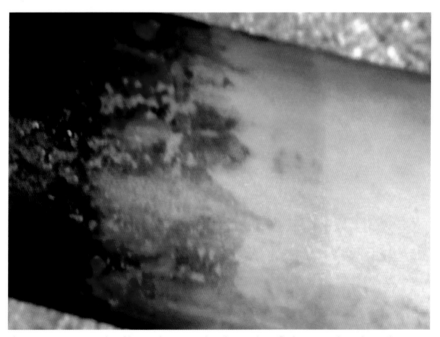

Figure 5.5. An example of burned mammalian bone identified in an archaeological assemblage, showing varying degrees of burning. Thick meat was likely present on the right side of this bone when it was burned.

Table 5.2. Stages of bone weathering (Adapted from Behrensmeyer 1978)

Stage	Description
0	No cracking or flaking. Bone is greasy. Skin and/or muscle ligaments may be attached.
1	Some cracking of bone surface. Skin or other tissue may or may not be present.
2	Cracking and flaking of bone surface. Only remnants of ligaments and cartilage may be present.
3	Surface has fibrous texture. Layers of bone may be gone. No tissue present.
4	Surface is coarse. Splinters fall from bone when moved.
5	Bone is fragile and may fall apart without being moved.

WEATHERED BONE

Weathered bone is bone that has been exposed to varying environmental conditions, such as changes in heat and moisture. These conditions cause the bone surface to change color and crack. Most weathered bone has been left at or near the ground surface for an extended period of time. Therefore, the presence and absence of bone weathering can provide a great deal of information on disposal or burial. For example, if the bone from a single feature contains a mixture of weathered and unweathered bone, it is likely that the weathered bone was originally left on the surface, maybe placed in a trash midden, and was later collected, along with fresh bone, to fill the feature.

The exterior of most weathered bone takes on a white appearance known as **sun bleaching**. A sun-bleached bone remained unburied for some period of time after it lost its natural moisture. The length of time necessary to bleach a bone white depends on the intensity of the exposure to the sun. Also common is surface cracking, which results when the brittle bone is exposed to changes in moisture, such as rain or snow, which cause the bone to repeatedly absorb and release water. The presence of surrounding plants increases the rate of cracking, as acids in plant roots etch the bone surface and masses of roots penetrate the bone, seeking moisture and nutrients. The marks that plant roots leave on bone are called **root etching**.

At a minimum any taphonomic analysis should document the presence or absence of weathering on each and every bone cataloged. A more detailed analysis should also note the type of weathering (sun bleaching, surface cracking, root etching). An exhaustive taphonomic analysis might classify each bone into stages of weathering, such as those developed by Behrensmeyer (1978). Table 5.2 summarizes those stages. Bone weathering is usually greatest on the upper surfaces, those most exposed to the sun, wind, and rain. Therefore, weathering may not have occurred uniformly over the entire bone surface.

GNAWED BONE

Bone that remains unburied for any period of time is also subject to alteration by animals, especially carnivores and rodents. For carnivores, the marrow in fresh bone provides nutrients. To reach the marrow, carnivores tend to focus their gnawing on the articular ends of bones. For rodents, gnawing on dry bone provides nutrients in the form of minerals, while wearing down their ever-growing incisors. If a rodent does not trim its incisors, they will continue to grow until the teeth pierce the animal's cranial bone, killing it. Although archaeologists tend to associate rodent gnawing with dried bones, rodents may also gnaw on fresh bones (Haglund 1997).

Carnivore gnawing and **rodent gnawing** produce distinct marks on the bone surface (figure 5.6). The rounder and more pointed shape of carnivore canines can produce **furrows** or **tooth pits**. Furrows are long scratches along the bone surface that taper to a point. These are created as a tooth scrapes along the bone surface and can appear in isolation or as a series of scratches that intersect at various angles. More common, however, are carnivore tooth pits. These are circular punctures of the bone surface made by the pointed teeth while an animal is gnawing on or carrying a bone. Because the size of a carnivore canine tooth varies from the small tip to the wide base, their tooth pits usually appear as a circle within a circle (see figure 5.6). Rodent gnawing is done not with pointed teeth but with square, chisel-shaped incisors. The paired incisors produce paired furrows that are shallow but long and relatively square in cross-section. Rodent gnawing is usually focused on the edges of bone, while carnivore gnawing is focused on the articular ends, where the spongy bone is found.

IDENTIFYING CARNIVORE AND RODENT GNAWING
- Carnivore tooth furrows—long scratches of the bone that end in a tapered point; may be isolated or occur as a series of scratches; tend to occur at or near articular ends of bone
- Carnivore tooth pit—circular puncture of bone; may appear as a circle within a circle; tends to occur at or near articular ends of bone
- Rodent tooth furrows—paired rectangular scratches of the bone surface that occur at thin areas of the edges of bone

---

It is important to note all evidence of carnivore and rodent activity, for both groups are capable of completely destroying a bone by gnawing, and both are known for removing bone to a secondary location such as a nest or den. Therefore, if there is any evidence of gnawing on the bones of your assemblage, your entire assemblage may have been altered by the action of these animals.

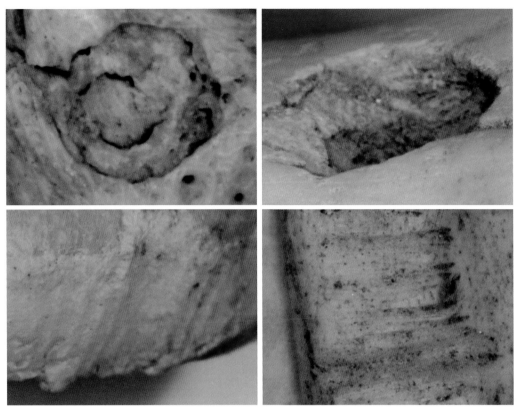

Figure 5.6. Four examples of gnawed mammalian bone identified in an archaeological assemblage. The top two images depict the circular depression created by the canine tooth of a carnivore. The bottom two images depict the square parallel striations of the paired incisors of a rodent. All were photographed at 50× magnification, which shows features not visible to the naked eye.

DIGESTIVE DAMAGE

Although some animals will get what they need by gnawing on bone, others will actually consume bone fragments. Occasionally these fragments find their way back out of the animal and into the archaeological record. Bones that have passed through a digestive system have a unique appearance. **Digestive damage** smoothes out the edges of a bone and creates the appearance of a surface polish (figure 5.7). This may be evidence of carnivore activity at the site, but the same digestive damage can occur if a bone is passed through a human or any other digestive system.

THE BIASED ASSEMBLAGE

As chapter 2 explains, just as all archaeological assemblages are **biased**, the bones that an animal bone analyst receives is always a biased sample of the animals that were once present at the site. For example, some bones are so

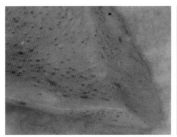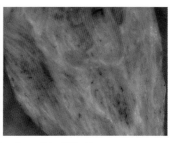

Figure 5.7. Three examples of digestive damage on mammalian bone identified in an archaeological assemblage, viewed with 50× magnification, which shows features not visible to the naked eye.

small that their recovery using standard archaeological techniques is unlikely. Others are so fragile that the field crew may not have been able to recover them without reducing them to small splinters of bone. Natural or cultural processes such as weathering or butchering may have destroyed some bone long before archaeological excavation began. Bones that were never collected by the field crew or never survived transportation from the field to the faunal analyst cannot be directly studied, but they are not completely out of reach of our analyses.

Bone-density studies provide us with a means of measuring the **density-mediated attrition** of an assemblage. This is an estimation of the impact of bone density on the **survivorship** of the bones that make up an assemblage. Essentially, we can assess what has been lost by documenting what is present. Thanks to some important studies, recording bone-density data is simple and can be done as the analyst catalogs each bone. It is not necessary to record these data for each and every bone; instead, select one or more common species, such as deer, dog, or rabbit, and record the required data for each deer, dog, or rabbit bone as it is cataloged.

Every animal bone is made up of portions that are more or less dense. Medical equipment, like that used to detect osteoporosis in humans, has been used to scan animal bones and measure the density of specific regions. These are known as **scan sites**. The resulting density data are published in figure and table format (e.g., Lam, Chen, and Pearson 1999; Lam et al. 2003; Novecosky and Popkin 2005; Pavao and Stahl 1999; Stahl 1999) and show what portion of the bone was scanned, along with the density reading for that scan site (figure 5.8).

To include bone-density data in your faunal catalog, simply determine whether the scan sites for a particular bone are present when you identify that bone. For example, if you are recording density data for rabbit bones and identify a rabbit femur, you would consult a diagram showing the different scan sites of rabbit femurs. Once that image has been obtained (you should have these images on hand when you start cataloging), compare it to the archaeo-

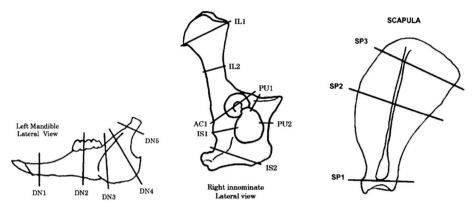

Figure 5.8. Examples of scan sites used to analyze density-mediated attrition. (Adapted from Novecosky and Popkin 2005; Pavao and Stahl 1999; and Stahl 1999.)

logical femur. If the proximal femur is missing, then you do not have those scan sites; record a value of 0 for those. If a midshaft scan site is only half present, record a value of 50 for it. If all distal articulation scan sites are present, record a value of 100 for each. These are your survivorship values for each scan site.

If you would like to conduct a study of the density-mediated attrition of your assemblage, I recommend consulting the studies cited earlier in this chapter and other more general studies on bone density (e.g., Lyman 1994, 256) for details on estimating survivorship within the assemblage. This is just one of many advanced faunal-analysis techniques that are covered in advanced zooarchaeology manuals (e.g., Reitz and Wing 2008; Lyman 1994, 2008). Most other advanced techniques do not require special forms of data collection like bone density. Instead, they use basic faunal data in creative ways to extract additional information such as season of death, approximate weight of meat obtained, and strategies for the transportation of fresh kills. Recording basic faunal data, therefore, is the key to a successful analysis.

6

Recording Your Data

Now that you have thought about what information you are going to gather from the assemblage, it is time to figure out how you are going to record it. There are many decisions to make. Will you use a paper catalog and then enter your data into a computer? Or will you enter your data directly into the computer? Will you use database or spreadsheet software? Will you use a coding system of numbers or letters, or will you type out full words? Will you enter all the data in one place or have separate files for different types of data?

These decisions are yours to make, for they will not affect the overall results of your analysis. Consider whether you have access to a computer while you are cataloging. If so, I recommend that you skip the paper stage and go directly to the digital system. If your assemblage is small (fewer than 2,500 bones), a spreadsheet program is usually sufficient. Larger assemblages are often easier to analyze with a database if you are comfortable using one. A coding system can be cumbersome unless you have it memorized, in which case it will save time. Keeping all of the data in one place is easier than managing different tables within a database or worksheets within a spreadsheet program, but your data can become overwhelming when they are all together. Again, your personal preference and comfort level with a specific system may dictate your choices.

There are more crucial aspects to recording your data to focus on. These concern the integrity and uniformity of your data and your ability to draw clear connections between your research questions, data, and conclusions. This means you need to be honest about the limitations of your abilities and data.

LEVELS OF CERTAINTY

Everyone wants to be able to pick up a bone and, regardless of its size or rarity, confidently declare exactly what species it represents. However, the truth is that it takes many years of experience to acquire these abilities. Those years are filled with hours spent amid comparative collections and published bone atlases in sometimes futile attempts to identify a single bone. While species-level identifications are always the goal, only a portion of any assemblage can be identified to that level.

Thanks to the hierarchical nature of taxonomy, failure to identify a bone to the species level does not equate to failure to identify the bone. Assume you have a portion of the tibia of an eastern gray squirrel *(Sciurus carolinensis)*. At this point you do not know it is from this exact species of squirrel, but you think it might be. To be certain, you should compare this tibia to not only that of a gray squirrel but also to those of other squirrels of similar size. How certain is your identification now?

If you are sure the tibia matches best with that of an eastern gray squirrel, then you should catalog it as such. If, however, there is not enough of your tibia to be sure, and especially if it also matches well with another squirrel species, such as the red squirrel *(Tamiasciurus hudsonicus),* then you should not catalog the tibia as an eastern gray squirrel. If you cannot say what species it is for certain, then you must catalog your tibia only as a squirrel (family Sciuridae). By doing so you are saying the tibia is certainly that of a squirrel. To try to push your identification to the species level would be misleading. Going up one or two levels in your taxonomy keeps you from being wrong.

Always strive to be the *least wrong* (most accurate) instead of the *most precise* in your identifications. Do not be lazy, either. If you are handed a rodent tibia and you know it is a rodent tibia, take the time to figure out how precise your identification can get. Can you determine the family, genus, or species? Some bones will stump you for days, but then, seemingly out of nowhere, you will have a breakthrough and identify them.

The same process works for identifying the bone to its skeletal element. If you have a fragment of spongy bone, it may be from a vertebra, a pelvis, or the articular end of any of the long bones. The best way to catalog this bone is simply as spongy bone. This is not a precise identification, but it is an accurate one. Fragments of cervical, thoracic, or lumbar vertebrae are often cataloged as vertebrae; fragments of humeri, radii, ulnae, femora, and tibiae are often cataloged as long bones; fragments of metacarpals and metatarsals are often cataloged as metapodials; and so on.

Let's return to the example of the squirrel tibia. It is possible for you to have an eastern gray squirrel tibia, but when you compare it to the single specimen in your comparative collection or the only illustration in your favorite bone atlas, you may not come up with a total match. Your specimen may be slightly larger or smaller or have a slightly different form. Just as with humans, no two eastern gray squirrels are exactly alike. Many factors go into determining the exact size and shape of an individual's bones. Age, sex, environment, nutrition, and genetics all play a part. Your squirrel tibia may not match that of an adult male squirrel from New York, but it may match that of a young adult female from Maryland.

You may be wondering how certain you need to be in your identification before you can enter your findings as data in the catalog. Here are some rules that I go by.

MAKING IDENTIFICATIONS WITH CERTAINTY

1. Reliable data is what you *know*, not what you think. Always check your intuition against a dependable source. No matter how many deer femurs you have seen in your lifetime, you should always compare the bone you think is a deer femur to an actual deer femur or a scale illustration of one. Do not get sloppy just to save time.

2. Exclusion is as important as inclusion. Sometimes figuring out what your bone *is not* is the simplest way to increase your certainty as to what it actually *is*. Check species lists for the other sites in the area. Check the geographic distributions of species in the state.

3. If you are going to make an unusual identification, you need to be 100 percent certain. Do not identify an Arizona gray squirrel tibia in an assemblage from New York unless you are positive it is an Arizona gray squirrel and not an eastern gray squirrel.

4. Ignore identifications made by others. Field bags and field notes are filled with the intuitions of others, and often these notes can lead you astray. I once spent days looking for a sheep skull that a field crew kept asking about only to discover that the pig cranium I had already identified had been mistakenly identified by the crew.

5. Do not make an identification just to avoid admitting you are not sure what it is. Every assemblage has its unidentifiables.

If you are new to animal bone identification, you may want to make a distinction between **unidentifiable bones** and bones that are **unidentified**. To label a bone *unidentifiable* is to declare that, regardless of effort, it cannot be identified. To label a bone as *unidentified* is to declare that it has eluded identification for now but that it may be identified with additional effort. That additional effort may be having someone else look at it or gaining access to another comparative collection.

UNIDENTIFIED VS. UNIDENTIFIABLE BONE

- Unidentified bone is one that requires analysis (or additional analysis) to identify.
- Unidentifiable bone is one that cannot be identified.

SIZE CLASSES

Often it is not possible to confidently identify a specimen to a taxonomic group below the level of class. In these cases a generic identification of mammal, fish, bird, amphibian, or reptile should be avoided if it is possible to estimate the body size of the animal from which the specimen derives. For example, a mammalian long-bone fragment may be better described as a *large* mammalian long-bone fragment. That suggests that the fragment is from a white-tailed deer *(Odocoileus virginianus)* or domestic cow *(Bos taurus)* instead of from a house mouse *(Mus musculus)* or a desert kangaroo rat *(Dipodomys deserti)*.

While there are some standards for defining size classes, you can develop your own groupings based on your assemblage and research questions as long as you provide definitions for each category. Although some people may consider a cat a medium-size mammal, others may see a cat as a small mammal. Some sources use live body weights to define their categories, but references to common species should also be included. Be careful to use sample species that have a consistent body size. Since dogs range in size from the Chihuahua to the Great Dane, "dog" is not a useful example for body-size categories. The following are some size categories used in other sources. Fish are difficult to ascribe to size groups since individuals of the same species can grow to vastly different body sizes.

BODY SIZE CLASSES

BIRDS
Tiny—finch or sparrow (< 50 grams [g] or 1.76 ounces [oz])
Small—thrush (50–100 g or 1.76–3.53 oz)
Medium—pigeon (100–400 g or 3.53–14.11 oz)
Large—chicken (400–3,000 g or 14.11–105.82 oz)
Very Large—goose (> 3 kilograms [kg] or 6.6 pounds [lbs])

MAMMALS
Size 1 or Small Mammal—rabbit (< 50 lbs or 22.68 kg)
Size 2 or Medium Mammal—pig (50–250 lbs or 22.68–113.40 kg)
Size 3 or Medium-Large Mammal—deer (250–750 lbs or 113.40–340.19 kg)
Size 4 or Large Mammal—cow (750–2,000 lbs or 340.19–907.18 kg)
Size 5 or Very Large Mammal—elephant (> 2,000 lbs or 907.18 kg)

MUTUALLY EXCLUSIVE CATEGORIES

Although the hierarchical nature of taxonomy comes in handy for providing levels of certainty, it can cause significant problems in the quantification (see chapter 7) and interpretation if mutually exclusive categories are not used. For example, say you identified twelve bones as follows: six rodents, five squirrels, and one gray squirrel. How many rodent bones do you have? The correct answer is twelve rodent bones. Rodent, squirrel, and gray squirrel are not mutually exclusive categories since all squirrels are rodents. Likewise, this assemblage contains six, not five, squirrel bones but only one gray squirrel bone. All gray squirrels are squirrels, but not all squirrels are gray squirrels.

The same issue can arise when quantifying your assemblage by skeletal element. For example, you identified twelve bones as follows: seven long-bone fragments, one femur fragment, and two phalanges. How many long bones do you have? The most accurate answer is that you have eight long-bone fragments. These may or may not be representative of eight actual long bones. To determine how many complete bones these eight fragments represent, you will need to have recorded data on the completeness of each specimen (see the following section, titled "Completeness and Articulations").

It is not necessary to use mutually exclusive categories when identifying your specimens. If your highest level of certainty says that one specimen is a gray squirrel tibia and another specimen is a rodent long bone, then that is how you should describe them in your catalog. Moreover, during the identification stage it is necessary to avoid using two different terms for the same exact thing, such as cataloging one rabbit incisor as an *incisor* and another as a *tooth*. If you are not sure that what you have is an incisor, go ahead and catalog it as a tooth. This records your highest level of certainty. However, if you are certain it is an incisor, you need to catalog it as such in order to be able to analyze it with the other rodent incisors.

This brings up an important methodological issue: If at all possible, the same analyst should perform all animal-bone identifications for a given archaeological assemblage. What one analyst may identify as a gray squirrel tibia, another may identify as a squirrel long bone. So when it comes to the data-analysis stage of the project, there will seem to have been more gray squirrel bones in one area of the site than in another, although the only real difference is the analyst. Similarly, one analyst may identify all vertebrae as vertebrae while another may break them down into the main groups (cervical, thoracic, lumbar, sacral, and caudal). A third analyst may take the time to determine exactly which vertebra each specimen is and catalog them as the first cervical, fifth thoracic, or third lumbar. Although it is not likely that the same individual will analyze archaeological assemblages from different years of excavation or different sites in the region, it is easier to recognize this bias when comparing two different data sets than to see it within one data set.

When comparing data sets from different analysts, you can use mutually exclusive categories to your advantage. Analysts are most likely to differ on their levels of certainty when it comes to very precise identifications. For example, based on experience or access to comparative resources, one analyst is likely to make more species-level identifications than another. Therefore, to make the data sets more comparable, you can simply reduce their data by one

Table 6.1. Comparison of several faunal assemblages from New York state by number of identified specimens (NISP)

Order	Lamoka-Madrigal	Scaccia	Frontenac Island	Lamoka-Guilday	Kipp Island	Sackett	*Engelbert-Beisaw
Carnivora	30	7	54	60	55	22	779
Rodentia	18	18	31	143	158	23	1,090
Lagomorpha		1		2	1		21
Artiodactyla	947	313	376	1,500	752	478	5,916
Podicipediformes				1			
Anseriformes	1	2	1	4	4	2	8
Falconiformes				2			
Galliformes	9	4	4	77	7	7	46
Columbiformes	12		1	274			10
Testudines	45	3	3	86	140	3	214
Squamata	3			2			814
Anura		6		6	29	102	4,371
Strigiformes							60
Ciconiiformes	1						
Charadriiformes							19
Insectivora							31
No. of Orders	9	8	7	12	8	7	13

* Some sites have been analyzed by several analysts. In those cases, the analyst's name appears after the site name. In this example the Engelbert site was described using the greatest number of taxonomic orders and is therefore the assemblage with the most richness.

or two levels of certainty while maintaining mutually exclusive categories. In other words, compare the two data sets after you have reduced all species-level identifications to the genus or family category they belong to. Count all gray squirrels as squirrels, and suddenly two seemingly different assemblages may be a lot more similar than they originally appeared (table 6.1). The same can be done for skeletal-element identifications. Table 6.1 uses the number of identified specimens (NISP) count, which is described in chapter 7.

If a specific project is likely to have different analysts cataloging their animal bones over the years, consider using a **relational database** from the beginning. In such a database it is possible to associate all gray squirrels with squirrels and rodents (create a relationship between them) so that you can automatically count all gray squirrels with all of your nonspecific squirrels when necessary without losing the original gray-squirrel identification. You can obtain a similar result when using a spreadsheet catalog by creating columns for each taxonomic level (class, order, family, genus, species) and populating all of the columns with each entry. This approach is more time consuming but requires less technical ability.

COMPLETENESS AND ARTICULATIONS

One simple way to make your database more **robust** (containing more useful data) is to always record the completeness of the identified specimen. For example, if your database says you have two gray-squirrel tibiae, how can you be sure these are not two portions of the same tibia without going through the time-consuming process of finding the specimens and trying to piece them together? If you have recorded the completeness of both specimens, this is an easy call to make.

A "completeness" field can be used to record how much of the overall bone is present. For example, the completeness field for a gray squirrel, right tibia may indicate that the bone is "50% complete." You may also have a second field called "articulation" to record which, if any, articular surface of the bone is present. For example, the entry for "gray squirrel, right tibia, 50% complete," now includes "distal articulation." This provides a very clear description of a specimen that contains the midshaft and distal articulation of the tibia. If a second gray squirrel tibia is cataloged as "right, 25% complete, proximal articulation," then these two specimens may be from the same tibia and should be counted as one tibia in the quantification stage. If, however, the second tibia is cataloged as "right, 75% complete, neither articulation," then the two specimens are mutually exclusive, as they contain overlapping portions of the midshaft, and would be counted as two tibiae (figure 6.1). Such data are crucial for determining the minimal number of individuals (see chapter 7) required to create the assemblage.

COUNTING AND WEIGHING BONE

Good faunal analysts know how to count their specimens. This may sound like the most straightforward aspect of identifying and analyzing animal bones, but it is often where an analysis goes wrong. For example, if one assemblage (A) has fourteen fragments of deer long bone and another assemblage (B) has twenty-six fragments of deer long bone, what can we say about our assemblages? Does assemblage B have more deer long bone than assemblage A? Can you tell by this count? What if the B fragments are all between three and four inches in length while those from assemblage A are five to eight inches in length? Does assemblage A have more deer long bone now? The most accurate statement about these two assemblages is simply that assemblage B has *more fragments* of deer long bone than assemblage A.

There are two ways to deal with the differences in fragmentation. My preferred method is to include a single weight for each and every line of data entry in my catalog. For example, if I enter fourteen white-tailed deer *(Odocoileus virginianus)* long-bone shaft fragments as a group into my database, I will weigh that group together and enter the combined fragment weight into the database in grams. That way if I want to compare the fourteen fragments from

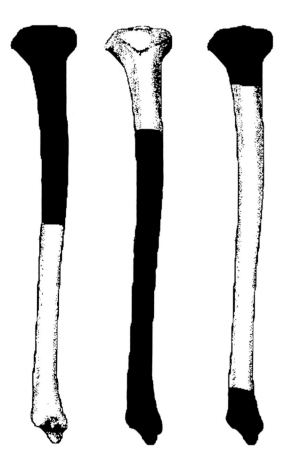

Figure 6.1. Example of how recording the completeness of a specimen can aid analysis. These tibia fragments were cataloged as 50 percent complete with distal articulation (left), 25 percent complete with proximal articulation (center), and 75 percent complete with neither articulation (right). The left and center specimens may be from the same tibia, while the specimen on the right must be from a second one.

this assemblage to the twenty-six from the other assemblage, I can determine the average size of the fragments in both groups using their total weights.

Grouping like specimens together into a single line of data saves quite a bit of time and is preferable to using a single line of data for each specimen. A good rule of thumb here is that if—and only if—all recorded information for any two specimens would be identical, then those specimens should be cataloged together. Of course, the count and weight fields are not considered in this comparison. The **context** (e.g., unit, stratum, feature) taxonomic identification, skeletal element identification, completeness, and taphonomic signatures must be the same (table 6.2). Avoid the temptation to lump together slightly different specimens.

If you are going to include bone weights in your catalog, you must ensure that all of your specimens are clean both inside and out (see chapter 2). Any adhering soil will skew your weights, and instead of differences in weight being reflective of bone size, the differences will be reflective of how clean or dirty your specimens are. A dog femur filled with sand can be heavier than a clean deer femur.

Table 6.2. Sample data showing how to use the count field to group similar specimens

Unit	Level	Genus	Species	Element	Side	Complete	Articulation	Modification	Count	Weight
39	F12b	Columba	livia	carpal	left	90%			2	0.1
39	F12b	Columba	livia	carpal	right	90%			5	0.1
39	F12b	Columba	livia	coracoid	left	fragment	distal		2	0.1
39	F12b	Columba	livia	coracoid	left	fragment	distal	charred	1	0.1

An alternative means of dealing with differences in fragmentation is to assign fragmentary bone to size classes. This technique is usually reserved for long-bone fragments and can provide data on bone breakage, whether for marrow extraction or as the result of **postdepositional** (after being deposited in the ground) taphonomic processes. The simplest way to assign fragments to size categories is to use nested screens. Each screen should have openings that are smaller than those in the one above it. For example, the top screen may have openings that are 4″ squares. The next screens have 3″ squares, 2″ squares, and 1″ squares. Bone specimens are placed on the top screen, and the stack of screens is agitated to encourage specimens to pass through each screen whose squares they can fit through. The stack of screens can then be separated, and the contents of each screen represent the number of specimens attributable to that size group.

The drawback of this simple technique is that if the openings in the screens have any sharp edges, they can scratch the bone surfaces and may thus obscure other taphonomic signatures, like butchery marks. For this reason, if the nested-screen approach is used, it should be done only after all other relevant data have been collected from the specimens. An alternative technique is to simply line up bone fragments lengthwise along a meter stick with those that are 1″–2″ in length lined up at the 1″ mark, those from two to three inches in length lined up at the 2″ mark, and so on. This approach is more time consuming but does not damage the specimens.

YOUR RESEARCH QUESTIONS

So far we have covered many different types of data that can be recorded for your assemblage. There are many more. For example, some analysts are using bone templates, either in simple paper form or within Geographic Information System (GIS) software (Abe et al. 2002), to record the exact shape of bone specimens and the exact placement of any taphonomic signatures. As previously mentioned, there are few standards in faunal analysis, and it is up to the analyst to decide what to record and how. Make this decision with your research questions in mind.

Before you record a single piece of data, divide a sheet of paper into two columns. Label the first column "What I Want to Learn" and the second "What Data I Need." Begin listing the goals of your analysis in the first column, and then ensure that each goal has at least one corresponding type of data in the second column. For example, if you want to learn about the use of wild species by the residents of a nineteenth-century farmstead, then in your data column you can write that you need to identify specimens to the species level. Is that all you need to learn about the use of wild species? You probably also want to include a butchery analysis of wild species in the data column. Do you want to learn about how these wild species were cooked? Were they roasted or boiled? If so, you want to include data about burning. Do you need to record data about fragmentation of long bones? Probably not.

Staying with this example, given the very focused research question posed, you may not even need to analyze the entire assemblage. You may need to look only for specimens of wild species and analyze those. Of course, this will mean you cannot compare the use of wild species to the use of domestic species at the site unless you collect the same data for both groups. The point is that research should be directed. New faunal analysts often get lost in trying to learn everything so that they can catalog one large assemblage. Instead, why not select a portion of the assemblage to work with in order to focus your efforts? Budding expert analysts have a lot to learn, but they do not need to learn it all at once.

COMMENT FIELDS

My last bit of advice about recording your data is to make liberal use of a "comments" field. I include one as the last field of data entry in all of my spreadsheet or database catalogs. This field contains any additional data that may be useful to me or to others who might use the data. It is an organized system of note taking.

No matter how much experience you have in analyzing bones, a few will always stump you. I often get that "I know what it is" feeling, but I just cannot place it. In cases like this I simply add the note "RECHECK" in the comments field and move on. Most assemblages are redundant in that they contain multiple specimens of the same bone. Therefore, at some point in the analysis of the remainder of the assemblage I will quite likely see that bone again, maybe broken a bit differently. That second specimen may be the key to identifying the earlier one. All I have to do then is to search my database for RECHECK in the comments field to figure out where that first specimen was and return to it for a final comparison.

The comments field is also a handy place to store any additional information about your specimens that you may want to track. For example, if you catalog an entire pig (Sus scrofa) mandible, but that mandible includes two molars, you can add "includes M2 (second molar) and M3 (third molar)" in the comments field. If your research questions warrant it, you may want to catalog these teeth separately from the mandible and then use the comments field to record "tooth located within mandible." I often use the comments field to keep track of mended bone in cases where the final count of my database will be much different from the inventory of bone specimens provided to me by a client. If I have reconstructed a white-tailed deer *(Odocoileus virginianus)* femur from five fragments, I catalog the femur as one bone and then add "mended from five fragments" in the comments field. If you find that you keep making the comments over and over in one catalog, this is a good indication that you should add a data entry field to cover that topic. For example, some of my catalogs have a field called "mended," which I populate with "yes" or "no."

7

Describing Your Data

Once your assemblage is cataloged, you will have a spreadsheet or database with a seemingly endless amount of variability within it. To make sense of it all, you need to describe the data and their variability with a few easy-to-use tools. These include some commonly used calculations, body-part profiles, and charts and graphs. As with all other aspects of animal-bone analysis, how you quantify your assemblage is up to you, but it should be informed by your research questions.

COMMON CALCULATIONS

Many books and articles are devoted to various techniques for quantifying animal-bone assemblages. Most of these methods rely on statistics and are specific to certain research questions, such as whether different portions of animals were transported to or away from the site or whether one species contributed more meat or other nutrients to the diet of the site inhabitants. Consult basic texts on zooarchaeology and taphonomy (e.g., Reitz and Wing 2008; Lyman 1994, 2008; Grayson 1984; Klein and Cruz-Uribe 1984) or journal articles for more information on the range of specialized statistics that are possible.

There are two basic statistics that all analysts should use to quantify their assemblages. These are the **minimum number of individuals (MNI)** and the **number of identified specimens (NISP)**, also known as the **total number of fragments (TNF)**. The MNI gives you the *minimum* number of individual animals of any given taxonomic group that would have been necessary to produce the specimens in your assemblage. The NISP gives you the *actual* number of specimens you identified as being within any given taxonomic group. For both of these statistics it is crucial to use mutually exclusive categories in order to avoid double counting specimens or individuals or missing them entirely.

NISP vs. MNI
- NISP is the actual number of bone specimens identified to a certain taxonomic group.

- MNI is the minimum number of individual animals of a specific taxonomic group that can account for the number of skeletal elements identified to that group.

The NISP is the simpler calculation and is done before the MNI. The NISP is usually just a tabulation of all specimens identified to a chosen taxonomic group. If your faunal catalog has nineteen specimens identified as white-tailed deer *(Odocoileus virginianus),* then the NISP for that species is nineteen. Recall the need to use mutually exclusive categories; a specimen should be counted as part of the most specific taxonomic group into which it was cataloged. For example, an eastern gray squirrel tibia would be counted as one specimen of *Sciurus carolinensis.* This specimen would not also be included in the count for its genus (*Sciurus* sp.), family (Sciuridae), or order (Rodentia). That said, you could include the eastern gray squirrel NISP in a total of *all* Rodentia if you wished; just be careful to make it clear that your NISP count is an **aggregate**, data that include the data of subgroups. To avoid confusion as to how the NISPs were calculated, many analysts present their data in table form (table 7.1) with the species-level categories indented under the genus-level categories and so on. Some also present a running total for the nested categories alongside the actual number for each category.

The MNI takes more time to calculate, but it provides more valuable data than the NISP. The NISP counts are biased by differences in fragmentation rates (see the earlier section titled "Counting and Weighing Bone" in this chapter). Moreover, MNIs are not biased, or at least not as seriously biased as NISPs. The MNI calculation is trying to find the minimum number of individuals of a particular group (e.g., species) required to create the assemblage. This is probably not the actual number of individuals that were once present; it is just the smallest number. In this way the MNI provides a much-needed reality check. Seemingly large assemblages that contain thousands of bone fragments can often be reduced to fewer than 100 individual animals. For example, the Nevada site used in table 7.1 has a total NISP of 227—that is, the entire assemblage comprised 227 bone fragments. However, after the MNIs were calculated, the assemblage can be explained as the result of only 7 individual animals at a minimum. This can tell us a lot about the duration of site habitation (days, not years), the very specific preferences of the site inhabitants (domestic species were obtained more often than wild ones), or the degree of fragmentation of individuals (cow bones were more fragmented than pig bones).

To calculate the MNI, first generate a list of specimens for each species identified. Included in this list should be the skeletal elements identified, the side of that element, the approximate age of the individual (juvenile vs. adult), the completeness of the bone, the presence of an articulation, and the total count.

Table 7.1. Sample faunal data from an archaeological site in Nevada showing how the NISP can be displayed as both independent and aggregate data

Class	Family or Genus	Common Name	NISP	MNI
Mammal	Artiodactyla	deer, sheep, pig	4 (26)*	
	Bos taurus	domestic cow	15	1
	Sus scrofa	domestic pig	7	1
	large mammal	cow size	27	
	medium mammal	pig size	30	
	medium/large mammal	pig to cow size	61	
	small mammal	rabbit size	5	1
Bird	*Phasianus colchicus*	ring-necked pheasant	3	1
	Gallus gallus	chicken	21	3
	medium Aves	chicken size	54	
Total			227	7

* The number in parentheses is an NISP. This is the aggregate NISP for all Artiodactyla, including the cow and the pig listed here.

Sort this list by skeletal element and side. Then look for all the paired elements, things that are represented by a left and a right on a complete skeleton, such as the humerus, femur, ulna, radius, and tibia. You can use any paired element, even the calcaneus or astragalus. Delete or cross off any data that are not from a paired element; do not use vertebrae, ribs, phalanges, and so on.

Next, determine how many lefts and how many rights of each paired element are represented by the data. The goal is to identify complete elements, so if there is one right humerus with only the proximal articulation and one right humerus with only the distal articulation, there is only one right humerus. Once you have calculated how many rights and how many lefts you have of each element, determine which element and which side are the most common. For example, if there are seven left humeri, six right humeri, six right femora, and five astragali, the left humerus is the most common. The count of the most common element and side gives you the minimum number of individuals of that species. Seven individual animals are needed to have had seven left humeri deposited in the assemblage. See table 7.2 for another example of how to calculate the MNI.

For mammals, MNI counts can be refined to take into account age differences of the individuals represented. To do this it is necessary to review the sequence of ossification for the species being quantified. For example, the proximal epiphysis of a domestic sheep *(Ovis aries)* humerus becomes fused to the shaft between 36 and 42 months of age (Silver 1963). The distal epiphysis of the same bone becomes fused around 10 months. Therefore, the fusion of the

Table 7.2. Sample Faunal Data from an Archaeological Site in Nevada Showing the Raw Data Needed to Calculate MNI

Genus	Species	Element	Side	Completeness	Articulation	Age	Count
Bos	taurus	femur	right	fragment	proximal	juvenile	1
Bos	taurus	femur	left	fragment	proximal	juvenile	1
Bos	taurus	humerus	left	fragment	proximal	juvenile	1
Bos	taurus	radius	right	fragment			1
~~Bos*~~	~~taurus~~	~~rib~~		~~fragment~~	~~absent~~		~~1~~
~~Bos~~	~~taurus~~	~~rib~~		~~fragment~~	~~absent~~		~~1~~
~~Bos~~	~~taurus~~	~~rib~~		~~fragment~~			~~1~~
~~Bos~~	~~taurus~~	~~rib~~		~~fragment~~			~~1~~
~~Bos~~	~~taurus~~	~~vertebra~~	~~axial~~	~~25%~~	~~distal~~	~~juvenile~~	~~1~~
~~Bos~~	~~taurus~~	~~vertebra~~	~~axial~~	~~fragment~~	~~distal~~	~~juvenile~~	~~1~~
~~Bos~~	~~taurus~~	~~vertebra~~	~~axial~~	~~75%~~	~~both~~	~~adult~~	~~1~~
~~Bos~~	~~taurus~~	~~vertebra~~		~~fragment~~	~~proximal~~	~~juvenile~~	~~1~~
~~Bos~~	~~taurus~~	~~cranial~~	~~axial~~	~~fragment~~	~~absent~~	~~adult~~	~~1~~
~~Bos~~	~~taurus~~	~~pubis~~		~~25%~~			~~1~~

*The crossed-out data cannot be used in the MNI calculation, as only paired elements (e.g., humerus, femur) are appropriate. A *Bos taurus* (domestic cow) MNI of 1 was calculated from the remaining data.

proximal articulation is more indicative of juvenile status. If your assemblage has three sheep humeri, two of which consist of a fused distal articulation and one of which consists of an unfused proximal articulation, what is the MNI? The most accurate MNI is two. If it is important for your research questions, you can break down the age groups as follows: One individual is between 10 and 42 months, and the other is greater than 10 months.

Another basic way to use NISP and MNI counts is to convert them to percentages by dividing any taxonomic group's MNI or NISP by the total MNI or NISP multiplied by one hundred. For example, the seven domestic dogs *(Canis familiaris)* would be 50 percent of the assemblage by MNI if the other animals include three woodchucks *(Marmota monax)* and two sheep *(Ovis aries)*. Percent MNI and percent NISP are shown in table 7.3. These data are from a large assemblage (NISP of 6,737) from Arizona. Looking just at NISP, this assemblage was mostly made up of bone fragments that could be identified only to size class, small and medium mammals. With the percentage of NISP we can quantify that 78.26 percent of the assemblage was made up of these small and medium mammal fragments. Converting MNI to percentages revealed that 22.57 percent of the assemblage's individuals (MNI) were hares (*Lepus* spp.) and rabbits (*Sylvilagus* spp.), while another 37.25 percent were various species of rodents. Table 7.3 also shows that MNI was not calculated for each and every taxonomic group identified. This is because of the need to maintain mutually exclusive categories (see chapter 6) to avoid double counting any individuals. For example, a bone that was identified only as that of a lagomorph may be a fragment of the same individual that was identified as a hare or a rabbit.

BODY-PART PROFILES

Because of taphonomic factors, we can expect to recover only a small portion of any animal that was utilized by our site inhabitants. In fact, if a complete or near-complete animal skeleton is recovered, it may have had nothing to do with the archaeological site under investigation. Animals die all the time, and their carcasses can accidentally become part of an archaeological assemblage. The exception, of course, occurs when animals are intentionally buried in graves, either alone or within a human grave.

Some animals are killed and butchered away from the site under investigation, and the only bones that have become part of the assemblage are those that have been transported back to a base camp or village. Animals that are killed and butchered in one place may still be incomplete because some bones are disposed of during the skinning process, others during the cooking process, and still others with the waste of a prepared meal. To understand which processes created the animal-bone assemblage, it is important to visualize which skeletal elements are present and which are absent for each genus or species identified. This can be done using body-part profiles.

A **body-part profile** begins with a sketch of the entire skeleton of a single species. Where possible, use a sketch of the animal in a natural position and with an outline drawing of the animal encompassing the skeleton. These drawings are analogous to an X-ray view. This allows nonspecialists to recognize the animal and the skeletal elements being depicted. This also allows the analyst to better visualize which elements should be recovered together based on butchery practices. Each bone of the skeleton should be clearly depicted.

Assemble sketches for each genus identified within your assemblage or just those that are relevant to your research questions. Once you have obtained the proper sketches, search the database or spreadsheet for the cataloged skeletal elements of each animal. Then simply shade in the cataloged elements on the sketch. For example, to produce a body-part profile for a domestic cow *(Bos taurus)*, determine which skeletal elements you cataloged as cow and then shade those elements in on a sketch of a cow skeleton (figure 7.1). If you desire very detailed skeletal-part profiles, use the completeness and articulation data to shade in only those portions of each bone that are present, and include the locations of cut marks. You may even want to list the total number of each skeletal element cataloged adjacent to that element on the sketch.

Table 7.3. An Example of How Percentage of Both NISP and MNI Can Help Quantify an Animal Bone Assemblage

Class	Species	NISP	% NISP*	MNI	% MNI
amphibian	*Anuran*	1	0.01		
amphibian	*Bufo* spp.	26	0.39	3	5.88
amphibian	Caudata	6	0.09	1	1.96
bird	*Bubo virginianus*	6	0.09	1	1.96
bird	*Buteo* spp.	1	0.01	1	1.96
bird	*Colinus virginianus*	1	0.01	1	1.96
bird	Galliforme	1	0.01		
bird	medium bird	62	0.92		
bird	Phasianidae	1	0.01		
bird	small bird	27	0.4		
bird	*Strix* spp.	2	0.03	1	1.96
bird	*Toxostoma rufum*	7	0.1	2	3.92
fish	small fish	1	0.01	1	1.96
mammal	Artiodactyla	23	0.34		
mammal	Canidae	5	0.07		
mammal	*Canis latrans*	1	0.01	1	1.96
mammal	Cervidae	11	0.16		
mammal	*Citellus spilosoma*	5	0.07	1	1.96
mammal	*Citellus variegatus*	1	0.01	1	1.96
mammal	*Cynomys* spp.	6	0.09	2	3.92
mammal	*Dipodomys* spp.	3	0.04	1	1.96
mammal	*Eutamias dorsalis*	1	0.01	1	1.96
mammal	Geomyidae	16	0.24	1	1.96
mammal	*Homo sapiens*	8	0.12	1	1.96
mammal	Lagamorpha	469	6.96		
mammal	large mammal	139	2.06		
mammal	*Lepus* spp.	198	2.94	9	17.65
mammal	medium mammal	1,259	18.69		
mammal	micromammal	87	1.29		
mammal	*Neotoma* spp.	11	0.16	3	5.88
mammal	*Odocoileus* spp.	1	0.01	1	1.96
mammal	*Onychomys leucogaster*	1	0.01	1	1.96
mammal	*Ovis canadensis*	1	0.01	1	1.96
mammal	*Perognathus apache*	3	0.04	2	3.92
mammal	*Peromyscus crinitus*	10	0.15	2	3.92
mammal	*Peromyscus maniculatus*	1	0.01	1	1.96
mammal	*Peromyscus* spp.	37	0.55		
mammal	*Reithrodontomys megalotis*	2	0.03	1	1.96
mammal	Rodentia	45	0.67		
mammal	Sciuridae	1	0.01		
mammal	small mammal	4,013	59.57		

Table 7.3. An Example of How Percentage of Both NISP and MNI Can Help Quantify an Animal Bone Assemblage (*continued*)

Class	Species	NISP	% NISP*	MNI	% MNI
mammal	*Sylvilagus* spp.	16	0.24	2	3.92
mammal	*Vulpes macrotis*	3	0.04	2	3.92
mammal	*Zapus princeps*	2	0.03	2	3.92
mollusc	Unid Mollusc	3	0.04	1	1.96
reptile	Crotalus atrox	197	2.92	1	1.96
reptile	Kinosternon spp.	5	0.07	1	1.96
reptile	Sauria	5	0.07	1	1.96
reptile	Serpentes	2	0.03		
reptile	Testudines	4	0.06		
Total		6,737		51	

*The data are from an archaeological site in Arizona. Each NISP was divided by the total NISP (6,737) and then multiplied by 100 to get the value for % NISP. The same was done for % MNI except that each MNI value was divided by the total MNI (51). MNI values are present only for the lowest level of a taxonomic identification due to the need to maintain mutually exclusive groups for that calculation.

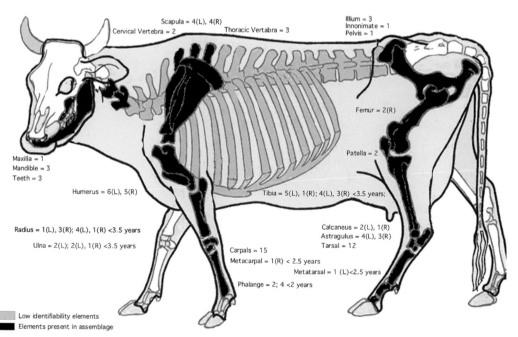

Figure 7.1. An example of a very detailed skeletal-part profile showing the elements of domestic cow *(Bos taurus)* that were recovered from a historic site in Colorado. In this case, information on the counts of each skeletal element are provided by side (L = left, R = right).

CONTEXTUAL ANALYSIS

Describing the assemblage as a whole allows for the general characterization of the site and its contents. However, most assemblages are composed of specimens from different contexts throughout the archaeological site. Those contexts that animal bones are most often recovered from are middens, **pit features** (holes dug into the ground that become filled with trash over time), and **burials** (holes dug into the ground to dispose of a body and other selected items and then filled quickly). Each of these contexts has its own taphonomic history, and therefore each context should be described separately.

The goal of this **contextual analysis** is to reveal patterns that may not be discernible when the assemblage is assessed as a whole. At a minimum, create a table for each context that lists the NISP and the MNI for each taxonomic group recovered from that feature. Be sure to use mutually exclusive categories and to recalculate the MNIs based only on those specimens recovered from the context being assessed. As such, each context is being treated as if it is an assemblage in itself. Once the table has been constructed, use text to describe this assemblage, including the taphonomic signatures of skeletal elements. Determine what percentage of this assemblage displays each taphonomic signature. If a large percentage displays the same taphonomic signatures, this is suggestive of an **activity area**, a location where a specific task was repeatedly performed. If a mixture of taphonomic signatures is revealed, then the assemblage is likely made up of refuse from a variety of activities.

After this descriptive exercise is repeated for each context, you may want to transform some of the textual information into bar charts in order to visually compare the contents of each context (figure 7.2). Take the contextual analysis a step further by linking your faunal database to a Geographic Information System to investigate spatial distributions of species, elements, or taphonomic signatures. These approaches will take your data far beyond the basic questions of what animals were used by the site inhabitants. An extensive contextual analysis can reveal patterns of site use as well as the formation processes that created the entire archaeological site.

PRODUCING A FAUNAL REPORT

A faunal report outlines the methods used to catalog an assemblage along with the recorded data, analysis, and basic interpretation. Since there are so few standards for indentifying and analyzing animal bone, the faunal report is a crucial record that should accompany every faunal catalog. (Links to several examples are provided in the online appendix.) It is often helpful to begin the report with some general information about the site or sites from which the assemblage derives and the exact dates of excavation that produced it. If only a subset of the assemblage was analyzed, this should be stated in the introduction so that it is clear to all of those who may wish to use the data. The intro-

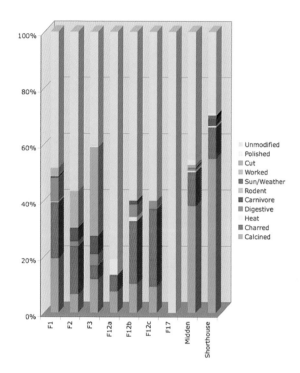

Figure 7.2. Bar chart showing what percentage of the bones within each site feature are unmodified (no taphonomic signatures) or modified by one of the taphonomic processes listed in the key on the right. This contextual analysis reveals that the bones from feature 17 (F17) are all unmodified, 50 percent of those from the short house are calcined, and 35 percent of those from feature 3 (F3) exhibit butchery cut marks.

Key: Unmodified, Polished, Cut, Worked, Sun/Weather, Rodent, Carnivore, Digestive, Heat, Charred, Calcined

duction is also a good place to define the terms you will be using. For example, some analysts do not differentiate between *charred* and *calcined* bone, referring to both as *burned* bone, while others may differentiate *completely calcined* (white) from *incompletely calcined* (gray or white with a black interior) bone.

The methods section, describing all of the methods used from the receipt of the assemblage up until its return, is recommended. This has proven useful when bags of bone are (or are thought to have been) misplaced and when returning to an analysis after a hiatus. Record the order in which the bags of bone are to be cataloged, such as by provenience or by bag number. This can help to recognize typing errors in the database. Record whether you assigned a unique identification number to each bone or bone bag or if you used numbers that were provided to you. Describe your procedure for dealing with nonbone, those bits of rocks, twigs, and ceramic that ended up in the assemblage: Did you separate them into new bags, leave them in their original bags, or discard them? Describe your procedure for dealing with worked bone and fragile specimens. State whether shell was analyzed. Document whether bone was cleaned, mended, or rebagged and how this was done. List any chemicals used.

Describe the resources used for taxonomic identification, such as the name and location of comparative collections or bone atlases on which your identifications relied. Describe how tentative identifications were handled and the types of taxonomic information that may be found in the comments field. For element identification, describe the categories used, including definitions of terms like *long bone,* and the categories used for completeness and articulation. If size groups were used, describe your groupings. If age and sex determinations were made, describe your criteria. List the species that were aged and sexed and the references used to make your determinations.

Describe the types of taphonomic signatures that were documented and the categories used for each. List any relevant resources. If worked bone was found, describe how it was handled in the catalog. If a typology like that for Arroyo Hondo Pueblo was used, describe it and provide a reference, such as "(Lang and Harris 1984)." Document your procedure for counting and weighing bone. Describe how similar bones were grouped in the catalog. Describe what additional information might be found in the comments field.

Finally, describe all of the analytical methods that you used. List the calculations you performed and detail how they were done. Include references for the less common techniques. Do not include the results of your analysis here.

The data section of the report provides a general characterization of your assemblage and the results of all analyses. Save the interpretation for the next section of your report, the conclusion. The primary data a reader will be looking for is what animals were identified, so begin with this. Then move into quantification, minimally MNI and NISP by site and context. Start from the most general information and move toward the most specific.

Remember that most archaeologists are not very familiar with animal taxonomy or the natural behaviors of specific species. Be sure to provide the common names of each and every taxonomic group along with their scientific names. For groups that are not easily definable or recognizable, list the common names of some typical species. For each taxonomic group in your catalog, provide some information about preferred diet and habitat, as well as breeding, hibernation, and migration cycles. This information may be useful to those who are working on other aspects of the site or seeking to interpret the site as a whole.

Place a table of your MNI results near the information on taxonomic groups so that readers can see how common each group is. This table may also include the NISP, or a separate table can be provided for those data. For both MNI and NISP, include a total at the bottom of the table. You may want to include columns for percentage of MNI and percentage of NISP for every taxonomic group.

If the report is describing a relatively small assemblage or if the assemblage was from a small site with few discrete contexts, include taphonomic information along with information on the taxonomic groups. For example, if 10 percent of the elk *(Cervus elaphus)* bones were charred, say so in the section on elk. However, since taphonomy is often also context specific (elk bones in and near hearths are more likely to be burned than those away from hearths), the best place for taphonomic information is under *contextual analysis.*

For contextual analysis, describe the contents of each context as if they were a discrete assemblage. You may wish to restrict your contextual analysis to features such as hearths or storage pits, or you may wish to describe the contents of specific soil layers. A good rule of thumb is to separately quantify any context that should have a unique depositional history. Therefore, if the site was excavated using **arbitrary levels** (a stratum equaled a specific depth of soil instead of a distinct soil type and color), a contextual analysis of each level is not very useful.

Providing MNI counts for each context is encouraged, but make it clear that these are different from the sitewide MNI counts. For example, if the sitewide MNI for pigeons *(Columba livia)* is 2, but pigeons were found in four different features, the MNI for each of these features is at least 1. Therefore the total MNI for pigeon may be 5 for contextual analysis but 2 for sitewide analysis.

If there are more than four contexts described in your contextual analysis, consider providing a summary that compares each context. This is especially useful if you documented numerous taphonomic signatures. Provide a chart or table of the total percentage of bones with a specific signature by context (see figure 7.2). This may reveal that the bones from one feature contain most of the butchered bone while another contains most of the burned bone. A similar chart or table showing the distribution of taxonomic group by context may reveal that one feature contains most of the fish bones while another contains most of the rodents.

Either in the general sitewide summary or in your contextual analysis, include sections for any additional analyses you performed. Provide the results of these analyses, and use visual aids whenever possible. Charts and graphs can usually summarize these types of data more concisely than text can.

The end of your report is the place to address your research questions using the data and interpretations provided earlier in the report. This section should also serve as both a summary and a conclusion. Do not introduce completely new information about your site or assemblage here. Any data or interpretations that prove important to your research questions should have been described in the prior sections.

If you do not have any research questions of your own and none have been provided to you, use the end of the report to point out any interesting data or trends that are obvious to you. This can be framed as "future research" and can include suggestions for additional analyses that may help to reveal additional patterns or relationships. For example, if you are aware of other assemblages of animal bone from similar sites, point those out to your readers. If an analysis of butchery practices was not requested, but you noticed significant butchery of the bones, recommend that this analysis be undertaken in the future.

Be sure to include the full references of any works that were cited in the report in a section called "references." Attach a copy of the faunal catalog to the report as an appendix. As space allows, include as many columns for data as possible. At a minimum be sure to have some provenience information, taxonomic identification, element, side, and count. After the catalog attach any figures that may be necessary to support the report in general. If the report is intended for someone with little knowledge of skeletal anatomy, consider attaching reference diagrams that identify the bones of nonmammals if any were found in the assemblage. Finally, include a copy of your résumé or curriculum vitae. This can be useful for several reasons. First, it documents the credentials of the analyst at the time the work was done. Second, if some time has passed, anyone who might wish to contact you can use the contents of your credentials to track you down.

A sample faunal report is included in the online appendix of this manual. Consider this a general guideline and not a standardized template. Your report will be more or less detailed depending on the scope of your project.

Epilogue

This manual presents the very basics of faunal analysis for the novice; cataloging an assemblage and writing up a basic report is just the beginning of a faunal analysis. A true faunal analyst will then take the data and apply them to research questions using a suite of analytical and interpretive techniques not covered here. Expert faunal analysts are creative in their use of animal-bone data to inform on far more than human diet. However, all experts have to begin somewhere, and I hope this manual helps to put a few people on that journey. Developing into an expert faunal analyst requires a significant amount of time reading the work of others and analyzing a wide range of animal-bone assemblages. There is no shortage of assemblages awaiting analysis.

Appendix 1 Online Appendix

Visit www.identifyingbones.com to access selected material from the book and supplemental resources.

MATERIAL FROM THE BOOK

- Tools of the Trade - Checklist
- Tips for identifying animal bone
- American species by habitat
- Enhanced figures

SUPPLEMENTAL INFORMATION

- Sample faunal data
- Sample faunal reports
- Research ideas
- Calculating richness and evenness
- Using bone density to calculate survivorship

Appendix 2 Bone Atlases

MAMMAL BONE ATLASES

Mammal Remains from Archaeological Sites (Olsen 1964)

Atlas of Animal Bones (Schmid 1972)

Mammalian Zooarchaeology, Alaska (Smith 1979)

A Key to Postcranial Skeletal Remains of Cattle/Bison, Elk, and Horse (Brown and Gustafson 1979)

An Osteology of Some Maya Mammals (Olsen 1982)

A Guide to Post-Cranial Bones of East African Animals (Walker 1985)

The Osteology of the South American Camelids (Pacheco Torres, Enciso, and Porras 1986)

Mammalian Osteology (Gilbert 1990)

Teeth (Hillson 1990)

Illustrated Key to Skulls of Genera of North American Land Mammals (Jones and Manning 1992)

Skulls and Bones: A Guide to the Skeletal Structures and Behavior of North American Mammals (Seafross 1995)

Mammal Bones and Teeth: An Introductory Guide to Methods of Identification (Hillson 1996)

FISH BONE ATLASES

Fish, Amphibian, and Reptile Remains from Archaeological Sites (Olsen 1968)

Marine Fish Osteology: A Manual for Archaeologists (Cannon 1987)

BIRD BONE ATLASES

Mexican Macaws: Comparative Osteology and Survey of Remains from the Southwest (Hargrave 1970)

Osteology for the Archaeologist (Olsen 1979)

A Manual for the Identification of Bird Bones from Archaeological Sites (Cohen and Serjeantson 1996)

Avian Osteology (Gilbert, Martin, and Savage 1996)

Identification of Waterfowl Breastbones and Avian Osteology (Sterna) of North American Anseriformes (Oates, Boyd, and Ramaekers 2003)

REPTILE BONE ATLASES

Osteology of the Reptiles (Romer 1956)

Fish, Amphibian, and Reptile Remains from Archaeological Sites (Olsen 1968)

A Turtle Atlas to Facilitate Archaeological Identification (Sobolik and Steele 1996)

AMPHIBIAN BONE ATLASES

Fish, Amphibian, and Reptile Remains from Archaeological Sites (Olsen 1968)

Appendix 3 Mammals, Fish, Birds, Reptiles, and Amphibians by Habitat Preference

Common Mammal Habitat Types

Desert—vegetation is sparse and rainfall is low

Forest—mostly tree vegetation

Grassland—mostly grass vegetation

Mountain—low vegetation at or near high elevations

Savanna—grassland with some scattered trees

Swampland—wetland with woody vegetation

Grassland Mammals of North America and South America

Antilocapra americana (pronghorn)—western North America

Bison bison (American bison)—western North America

Canis latrans (coyote)—North America and Central America

Cervus elaphus (elk or red deer)—Northern Hemisphere

Cynomys leucurus (white-tailed prairie dog)—western North America

Dasypus novemcinctus (nine-banded armadillo)—North America and South America

Dipodomys ordii (Ord's kangaroo rat)—western North America

Erethizon dorsatum (North American porcupine)—North America

Geomys bursarius (Plains pocket gopher)—western North America

Lama guanicoe (guanaco)—western South America

Lama pacos (alpaca)—western South America

Lepus californicus (black-tailed jackrabbit)—southwestern North America

Lepus townsendii (white-tailed jackrabbit)—northwestern North America

Lynx rufus (bobcat)—North America

Mustela nigripes (black-footed ferret)—North America

Neotoma floridana (eastern wood rat)—eastern North America

Neovison vison (American mink)—North America

Odocoileus hemionus (mule deer)—western North America

Onychomys leucogaster (northern grasshopper mouse)—western North America

Perognathus flavescens (Plains pocket mouse)—central North America

Peromyscus maniculatus (deer mouse)—North America

Procyon lotor (northern raccoon)—North America to northern South America

Puma concolor (cougar or mountain lion)—North America and South America

Reithrodontomys megalotis (western harvest mouse)—western North America

Sigmodon arizonae (Arizona cotton rat)—southern North America to northern South America

Spermophilus variegatus (rock squirrel)—southwestern North America

Sylvilagus audubonii (desert cottontail)—southwestern North America

Taxidea taxus (American badger)—central North America

Urocyon cinereoargenteus (gray fox)—southern North America and Central America

Ursus arctos (brown bear)—Northern Hemisphere

Vicugna vicugna (vicuña)—western South America

Vulpes vulpes (red fox)—Northern Hemisphere

Zapus hudsonius (meadow jumping mouse)—eastern North America

Zapus princeps (western jumping mouse)—western North America

Forest Mammals of North America and South America

Alces alces (Eurasian elk)—northern North America and Europe

Alces americanus (moose)—northern North America

Canis latrans (coyote)—North America and Central America

Canis lupus (gray wolf)—Northern Hemisphere

Castor canadensis (American beaver)—North America

Cervus elaphus (elk or red deer)—Northern Hemisphere

Dasypus novemcinctus (nine-banded armadillo)—North America and South America

Didelphis virginiana (Virginia opossum)—North America and Central America

Erethizon dorsatum (North American porcupine)—North America

Lepus americanus (snowshoe hare)—northern North America

Lepus townsendii (white-tailed jackrabbit)—northwestern North America

Lynx canadensis (Canada lynx)—northern North America

Lynx rufus (bobcat)—North America

Marmota monax (woodchuck)—North America

Mephitis mephitis (striped skunk)—North America

Mustela frenata (long-tailed weasel)—North America to northern South America

Neotoma floridana (eastern wood rat)—eastern North America

Neotoma lepida (desert wood rat)—western North America

Neotoma mexicana (Mexican wood rat)—southwestern North America and Central America

Neovison vison (American mink)—North America

Odocoileus hemionus (mule deer)—western North America

Odocoileus virginianus (white-tailed deer)—North America and Central America

Peromyscus maniculatus (deer mouse)—North America

Procyon lotor (northern raccoon)—North America to northern South America

Puma concolor (cougar or mountain lion)—North America and South America

Rangifer tarandus (caribou)—Circumpolar

Reithrodontomys megalotis (western harvest mouse)—western North America

Sciurus carolinensis (eastern gray squirrel)—eastern North America

Sciurus niger (eastern fox squirrel)—eastern and central North America

Sigmodon arizonae (Arizona cotton rat)—southern North America to northern South America

Sylvilagus floridanus (eastern cottontail)—eastern North America and northwestern South America

Tamias striatus (eastern chipmunk)—eastern North America

Tamiasciurus hudsonicus (red squirrel)—North America

Urocyon cinereoargenteus (gray fox)—southern North America and Central America

Ursus americanus (American black bear)—North America

Ursus arctos (brown bear)—Northern Hemisphere

Vulpes vulpes (red fox)—Northern Hemisphere

Mountain Mammals of North America and South America

Alces alces (Eurasian elk)—northern North America and Europe

Canis latrans (coyote)—North America and Central America

Canis lupus (gray wolf)—Northern Hemisphere

Cervus elaphus (elk or red deer)—Northern Hemisphere

Erethizon dorsatum (North American porcupine)—North America

Lama glama (llama)—western South America

Lama pacos (alpaca)—western South America

Lepus townsendii (white-tailed jackrabbit)—northwestern North America

Lynx rufus (bobcat)—North America

Neotoma mexicana (Mexican wood rat)—southwestern North America and Central America

Odocoileus hemionus (mule deer)—western North America

Oreamnos americanus (mountain goat)—northwestern North America

Ovis canadensis (bighorn sheep)—western North America

Peromyscus maniculatus (deer mouse)—North America

Puma concolor (cougar or mountain lion)—North America and South America

Reithrodontomys megalotis (western harvest mouse)—western North America

Taxidea taxus (American badger)—central North America

Ursus arctos (brown bear)—Northern Hemisphere

Vulpes vulpes (red fox)—Northern Hemisphere

Zapus hudsonius (meadow jumping mouse)—eastern North America

Desert Mammals of North America and South America

Antilocapra americana (pronghorn)—western North America

Canis latrans (coyote)—North America and Central America

Cynomys leucurus (white-tailed prairie dog)—western North America

Dipodomys ordii (Ord's kangaroo rat)—western North America

Erethizon dorsatum (North American porcupine)—North America

Lepus californicus (black-tailed jackrabbit)—southwestern North America

Lepus townsendii (white-tailed jackrabbit)—northwestern North America

Lynx rufus (bobcat)—North America

Neotoma lepida (desert wood rat)—western North America

Odocoileus hemionus (mule deer)—western North America

Onychomys leucogaster (northern grasshopper mouse)—western North America

Ovis canadensis (bighorn sheep)—western North America

Perognathus flavescens (Plains pocket mouse)—Central North America

Peromyscus maniculatus (deer mouse)—North America

Puma concolor (cougar or mountain lion)—North America and South America

Reithrodontomys megalotis (western harvest mouse)—western North America

Sylvilagus audubonii (desert cottontail)—southwestern North America

Taxidea taxus (American badger)—central North America

Ursus arctos (brown bear)—Northern Hemisphere

Vulpes vulpes (red fox)—Northern Hemisphere

FISH, BIRDS, REPTILES, AND AMPHIBIANS BY HABITAT PREFERENCE

Common Fish Habitat Types

Freshwater—water that lacks salt as is found in lakes, ponds, rivers, and streams

Brackish water—water with moderate salt as is found in coastal marshes

Saltwater—water with significant levels of salt as is found in oceans and seas

Freshwater Fish of North America

Alosa pseudoharengus (alewife or herring)—northeastern North America

Ameiurus melas (black bullhead)—North America

Ameiurus natalis (yellow bullhead)—eastern North America

Amia calva (bowfin)—eastern North America

Aplodinotis grunniens (freshwater drum)—eastern North America

Atractosteus spatula (alligator gar)—eastern North America

Esox lucius (northern pike)—North America and Eurasia

Ictalurus punctatus (channel catfish)—northern North America

Lepisosteus oculatus (spotted gar)—eastern North America

Lepisosteus osseus (longnose gar)—eastern North America

Lepisosteus platostomus (shortnose gar)—eastern North America

Lepisosteus platyrhincus (Florida gar)—eastern North America

Micropterus dolomieu (smallmouth bass)—eastern North America

Micropterus salmoides (bigmouth bass)—eastern North America

Morone chrysops (white bass)—North America

Oncorhynchus keta (Pacific salmon)—North Pacific

Oncorhynchus mykiss (rainbow trout)—western North America

Perca flavescens (yellow perch)—eastern North America

Salmo salar (Atlantic salmon)—North Atlantic

Brackish Water Fish of North America

Atractosteus spatula (alligator gar)—eastern North America

Gadus morhua (Atlantic cod)—North Atlantic

Ictalurus punctatus (channel catfish)—northern North America

Lepisosteus oculatus (spotted gar)—eastern North America

Lepisosteus platyrhincus (Florida gar)—eastern North America

Oncorhynchus mykiss (rainbow trout)—western North America

Saltwater Fish of North America

Alosa pseudoharengus (alewife or herring)—northeastern North America

Clupea harengus (Atlantic herring)—northern Atlantic

Clupea pallasii (Pacific herring)—northern Pacific

Gadus morhua (Atlantic cod)—North Atlantic

Hippoglossus hippoglossus (Atlantic halibut)—Atlantic

Hippoglossus stenolepis (Pacific halibut)—Pacific

Lepisosteus osseus (longnose gar)—eastern North America

Oncorhynchus keta (Pacific salmon)—North Pacific

Oncorhynchus mykiss (rainbow trout)—western North America

Pogonias cromis (black drum)—eastern North America

Salmo salar (Atlantic salmon)—North Atlantic

Sebastes caurinus (copper rockfish)—western North America

Sebastes marinus (red rockfish or red snapper)—Pacific

Theragra chalcogramma (Alaska pollock)—northern Pacific

Waterfowl, Seabirds, and Shorebirds

Aix sponsa (wood duck)—summer: North America; winter: southern North America

Anas discors (blue-winged teal)—summer: North America; winter: southern North America and South America

Anas platyrhynchos (mallard)—worldwide

Ardea herodias (great blue heron)—summer: North America and Central America; winter: North, Central, and South America

Branta canadensis (Canada goose)—summer: northern North America; winter: southern North America

Fulica americana (American coot or mud hen)—summer: northern North America; winter: southern North America

Gavia immer (common loon)—summer: northern North America; winter: North America

Larus californicus (Californian gull)—western North America

Pandion haliaetus (osprey)—worldwide

Pelecanus erythrorhynchos (American white pelican)—summer: inland North America; winter: coastal southern North America

Podiceps auritus (horned grebe)—summer: northern North America; winter: North America

Birds of Prey

Bubo virginianus (great horned owl)—North America and South America

Buteo jamaicensis (red-tailed hawk)—North America and Central America

Cathartes aura (turkey vulture)—North America and South America

Haliaeetus leucocephalus (bald eagle)—North America

Tyto alba (barn owl)—worldwide

Game Birds

Bonasa umbellus (ruffed grouse)—forests of North America

Colinus virginianus (northern bobwhite)—forests and grasslands of North America and Central America

Meleagris gallopavo (wild turkey)—forests of North America

Common Birds

Columba livia (common pigeon)—worldwide

Corvus brachyrhynchos (American crow)—North America

Corvus corax (common raven)—worldwide

Reptiles

Chelydra serpentina (snapping turtle)—eastern North America—fresh or brackish water

Chrysemys picta (painted turtle)—North America—freshwater

Crotaphytus collaris (collared lizard)—western North America—rock outcrops

Gopherus polyphemus (gopher tortoise)—southeastern North America—desert or forest

Kinosternon flavescens (yellow mud turtle)—central North America—freshwater

Pseuduemys concinna (river cooter)—eastern North America—fresh or brackish water

Sternotherus odoratus (common musk turtle)—eastern North America—freshwater

Terrapene Carolina (box turtle)—eastern North America—forest or grassland

Common Amphibians

Ambystoma tigrinum (tiger salamander)—North America—forest and grassland

Bufo americanus (American toad)—North America—all

Rana catesbeiana (North American bullfrog)—North America—all (water dependent)

Rana pipiens (northern leopard frog)—North America—grassland and forest

Spea bombifrons (plains spadefoot toad)—North America—desert and grassland

Glossary

accurate. Correct.

acetabular. Of the acetabulum.

acetabulum (pl. acetabula). Articulation of the innominate with the proximal femur, point on the innominate where the ilium, ischium, and pubis all come together.

Acipenseriformes. Taxonomic order of paddlefish and sturgeons.

acrodont. Having teeth that are part of the jawbone.

acromion. Process of the scapula found in some mammals.

Actinopterygii. Taxonomic class of ray-finned fishes.

activity area. A location where a specific task was repeatedly performed.

adult. A mature animal, one whose bones are fully formed and fully grown.

aggregate. Data that include the data of subgroups.

Amphibia. Taxonomic class of amphibians.

anataxic. Process that limits the animals that can end up in an assemblage based on how the bones were reexposed to weathering and other alterations after burial at a given time and place.

Animalia. Taxonomic kingdom of animals.

Anseriformes. Taxonomic order that includes ducks, geese, and swans.

anterior. Toward the front.

Antilocapridae. Taxonomic family of pronghorn antelope.

antitrochanter. Projection of the acetabulum of birds.

antlers. Bony projection of the cranium, shed and regrown every season, covered by soft velvetlike skin while the animal is alive.

Anura. Taxonomic order of frogs and toads.

appendicular skeleton. Bones of the appendages, the arms and legs.

arbitrary levels. A stratum equaled a specific depth of soil instead of a distinct soil type and color.

articular facet. Small and flat depression for articulation with another bone.

articulate. To come together or join.

articulations. Joints, where bones come together, marked by smooth bone.

Artiodactyls. Hoofed herbivores and omnivores, have teeth that are adapted for a varied diet, have an even number of toes.

assemblage. Collection of objects from an archaeological site.

astragalus (pl. astragali). Tarsal bone, allows the heel to move up and down.

atlas. The first cervical vertebra, which holds up the cranium.

Aves. Taxonomic class of birds.

axial skeleton. Bones of the head to pelvis, not including the arms and legs.

axis. The second cervical vertebra, which allows the cranium to rotate.

baculum. Penis bone, found in some carnivores, rodents, and primates.

basicranium. Base of the cranium, where the head meets the cervical vertebrae.

basipterigium. Bone of the pelvic girdle of a fish.

bias. Selective removal of some bones from the data set.

biotic. Relating to the process that limits the animals that can end up in an assemblage based on what animals are available at a given time and place.

blade. Thin, flat projection of bone.

body-part profile. Graphical means of displaying what bones are part of an assemblage using illustrations that are specific to a genus or species.

bone atlases. Books that illustrate the complete bones of specific animals.

Bovidae. Taxonomic family that includes bison, cow, sheep, and goats.

Bovinae. Taxonomic subfamily of Bovidae with spiral horns.

brachyodont. Having low-crowned (short) teeth.

bunodont. Having teeth with rounded cusps.

burials. Holes dug into the ground to dispose of a body and other selected items and filled quickly.

calcaneus. Tarsal bone; forms the heel.

calcined. Burned white; used here in reference to bone.

Camelidae. Taxonomic family that includes camels, llamas, and vicunas.

Canidae. Taxonomic family that includes dogs.

canines. Teeth between incisors and premolars; pointed teeth with one root.

Caprinae. Taxonomic subfamily of Bovidae with rear-projecting short horns.

carapace. Top shell of a turtle or tortoise.

carcass. Body of a dead animal.

Carnivora. Taxonomic order of carnivores.

carnivore gnawing. Marks created when a carnivore gnaws on a bone.

carnivore. Animal whose dietary preference is to consume animal tissue.

carpals. Small, compact bones of the wrist.

carpometacarpus. Fused carpals and metacarpals of a bird.

cataloging. Keeping a detailed inventory of a faunal assemblage.

caudal. At or close to the tail or the posterior of a body; opposite of **cranial.**

caudal vertebrae. Vertebrae of the tail, located after the sacrum or sacral vertebrae.

Caudata. Taxonomic order of salamanders.

centrum (pl. centra). Solid body of a vertebra, weight-bearing section of vertebrae.

Cephalophinae. Taxonomic subfamily of Bovidae with small horns.

cervical vertebrae. Vertebrae of the neck, located between the cranium and the thoracic vertebrae.

Cervidae. Taxonomic family that includes deer, elk, and moose.

Charadriiformes. Taxonomic order of shorebirds.

charred bone. Bone that has been burned black.

Chiroptera. Taxonomic order of bats.

Chordata. Taxonomic phylum of animals with a spinal cord.

class. Taxonomic level between phylum and order; this book is concerned with the classes of Mammalia, Actinopterygii, Sarcopterygii, Aves, Reptilia, and Amphibia.

clavicle. Bone that connects the humerus and scapula to the thorax.

coccyx. A structure created by the fusion of multiple caudal vertebrae.

Columbiformes. Taxonomic order of doves and pigeons.

commensals. Animals that live around humans and benefit from them.

comparative collections. Collections of real animal skeletons.

compression fracture. Type of bone break in which the bone has been crushed by direct or indirect percussion.

concave. Cupped or C shaped.

condyles. Rounded articular surfaces.

context. The unit, stratum, or feature from which a bone comes.

contextual analysis. Analysis of the subsets of a faunal assemblage based on the context in which the bones were recovered.

convex. Opposite of **concave**, projecting or D shaped.

coracoid. Bone of the shoulder girdle; in some animals the coracoid is part of the scapula.

coracoid process. Process of the scapula that helps form the shoulder joint in some mammals.

coronoid process. Process of the proximal ulna that forms the bottom of the hooklike articulation.

cortex. Exterior wall of a bone.

cranial. Relating to the cranium or skull; also used to indicate a part of the body that is closer to the head; opposite of **caudal**.

cranium. The bones of the braincase and face; together with the mandible it forms the skull.

crest. Long thin ridge of bone.

Crocodylia. Taxonomic order that includes crocodiles and alligators.

crown. Exposed enamel of the premolars and molars, the portion of the tooth that is above the gumline.

ctenoid scales. Round scales with pointed projections on one border.

cycloid scales. Thin, fan-shaped scales.

Cyprinidae. Taxonomic family of carps and minnows.

Cypriniformes. Taxonomic order of minnows and suckers.

database. Computer program used to hold the faunal catalog.

dens. Articular projection from the axis that allows for rotation.

density-mediated attrition. Impact of bone density on the survivorship of the bones that make up an assemblage.

dental formula. Numbers of each type of tooth as they are found in the mouth of a single species; the formula is written as a set of four numbers above and below a line; the top numbers represent the numbers of incisors, canines, premolars, and molars in the maxilla; the bottom numbers represent the same for the mandible.

dentary. Bone of the lower jaw in nonmammals; the equivalent of the mandible in the mammal skeleton.

dentition. Teeth.

desert. Habitat of sparse vegetation where rainfall is low.

digestive damage. A smoothing of the bone surface that occurs after a bone fragment has been through the digestive system of an animal.

digits. Bones of animals that are the equivalent of fingers or toes in the human skeleton.

diploë. Spongy bone of the cranium.

direct percussion. Force applied to a bone, as in hitting it directly with a hammer.

distal. Situated away from the top and center of a body; opposite of **proximal**.

domestic. In this volume, relating to animals that live with humans due to human intention.

dorsal. Relating to the upper side or back of a body when the body is in its normal anatomical position.

dorsal vertebrae. Vertebrae that articulate with ribs in a snake skeleton.

epiphyseal fusion. The timing of the fusion of the epiphyses to the shaft.

epiphyses. Unfused ends of long bones.

Falconiformes. Taxonomic order of the diurnal birds of prey, includes eagles, hawks, and falcons.

faunal analysis. Animal-bone analysis.

Felidae. Taxonomic family of cats.

femoral. Relating to the femur.

femur (pl. femora). Thigh bone; bone of the lower limb that articulates with the pelvis.

fibula (pl. fibulae). Bone of the lower limb that articulates with the tibia; on the lateral side.

foramen (pl. foramina or foramens). A hole in a bone.

foramen transversarium. Holes found in cervical vertebrae, one on each side of the small centrum.

forest. Habitat of mostly trees and undergrowth.

fossa. Depression of the bone surface.

fovea capitis. Small oval to circular depression found on the head of the femur.

functional morphology. A field of study that holds that the shape of an animal's bones is determined by their function.

furcula. Wishbone of the bird skeleton; fused clavicles.

furrows. Long scratches along a bone surface.

Galliformes. Taxonomic order that includes pheasants, quails, and chickens.

ganoid scales. Thick, diamond-shaped scales.

Gaviiformes. Taxonomic order of loons and divers.

glenoid cavity. Same as glenoid fossa.

glenoid fossa. Depression of the lateral scapula that articulates with the proximal humerus.

grassland. Habitat with mostly grass vegetation.

greater trochanter. Projection of bone on the lateral proximal femur for muscle attachment.

greenstick fractures. Type of bone break that involves some bending or deformation of the bone; this occurs only if the bone was broken when it was still moist or fresh.

head. Round knob of bone, such as the proximal head of the femur.

hemal spine. Ventral projection of the vertebra in fish, opposite the neural spine; same as **haemal spine**.

hemimandible. One side of a mandible.

hens. Female domestic birds.

herbivores. Animals whose dietary preference is to consume plant tissue.

Hippotraginae. Taxonomic subfamily of Bovidae with ringed horns.

horns. Bony projections of the cranium that continue to grow throughout the life of an animal; covered by a hard material of keratin and other proteins while the animal is alive.

humerus (pl. humeri). Bone of the upper limb; articulates with the scapula and the radius and ulna.

hypapophyses. Small, thin projections of bone that point caudally; found on some bird vertebrae.

hypercoracoid. Bone of the fish skeleton's shoulder girdle, situated above the hypocoracoid.

hypocoracoid. Bone of the fish skeleton's shoulder girdle, situated below the hypercoracoid.

hypsodont. Having high-crowned (tall) teeth.

ilium (pl. ilia). The bone of the pelvis that projects cranially from the acetabulum.

incisors. Front teeth of mammals; flat in profile and have only one root.

indirect percussion. Force applied to a bone by hitting an object placed between the bone and the hammer.

innominate. A fused ilium, ischium, and pubis; two innominates fuse to a sacrum to create a pelvis in mammals; same as os coxa.

insectivore. Animal whose dietary preference is to consume insects.

ischium. The bone of the pelvis that projects caudally from the acetabulum.

juvenile. An immature animal, one whose bones are not yet fully formed or fully grown.

kingdom. Most general level of taxonomy; this book is concerned with the kingdom of Animalia.

knife cuts. Marks created when a cutting edge is dragged across a bone surface.

lagomorph. A member of the taxonomic order Lagomorpha.

Lagomorpha. Taxonomic order of hares, pikas, and rabbits.

lateral. Situated away from the axial skeleton; opposite of **medial**.

Leporidae. Taxonomic family of hares and rabbits.

lesser trochanter. Projection of bone on the medial proximal femur for muscle attachment.

long bone. Bone with a long shaft, such as the humerus and femur.

lophodont. Having teeth with ridges between cusps.

lumbar vertebrae. Vertebrae of the lower back between the thoracic and sacral vertebrae or sacrum.

Mammalia. Taxonomic class of mammals.

mandible. Lower jaw bone; together with the cranium it forms the skull.

mandibular condyle. A process on the mandible that articulates with the cranium.

mandibular teeth. Teeth found in the mandible.

manus. Bones of the hand.

marrow. Calorie-rich fatty substance found in the shaft of long bones.

maxilla (pl. maxillae). Upper portion of the jaw that is part of the cranium.

maxillary teeth. Teeth found in the maxilla.

medial. Situated near the axial skeleton; opposite of **lateral**.

medial malleolus. Landmark on the distal tibia; forms part of the ankle joint.

medullary bone. Deposits that can be found inside the long bones of birds who are laying eggs; resembles a white or light-colored stuffing.

metacarpals. Bones that sit between the carpals and the phalanges, forming the palm in humans.

metapodials. Collective term for the bones of the wrists, ankles, hands, and feet.

metatarsals. Bones that sit between the tarsals and the phalanges, forming the ball of the foot in humans.

midden. Trash heap.

migratory species. Species of animals that live in different regions at different times of the year.

minimum number of individuals (MNI). The fewest individual animals of a specific taxonomic group that can account for the number of skeletal elements identified to that group.

molars. Teeth at the back of the mouth, after the premolars; complex crowns with one or more roots.

Moschidae. Taxonomic family that includes musk deer.

mountain. Habitat at or near high elevations that consists of mostly low vegetation.

Mustelidae. Taxonomic family that includes badgers, otters, and weasels.

neck. Narrow segment of bone below the head, as in the neck of the femur.

neural arch. The structure that projects from the centrum of a vertebra and encases the spinal cord.

neural spine. Dorsal projection of the vertebra in fish; same as the spinous process in other animals.

New World. North America and South America.

nonbone. Bits of rocks, twigs, and ceramic in an assemblage.

notarium. Fused thoracic vertebrae in a bird.

number of identified specimens (NISP). The actual number of bone specimens identified to a certain taxonomic group.

nutrient foramina. Holes that transport nutrients to the inner bone cavity.

obturator foramen. The foramen created by the pubis (medially) and the ischium (laterally).

Ochotonidae. Taxonomic family of pikas.

odontoid process. Same as dens; articular projection from the axis that allows for rotation.

Old World. Europe, Asia, and Africa.

olecranon process. Process of the proximal ulna that forms the top of the hooklike articulation.

omnivore. Animal whose dietary preference is to consume a variety of foods, both plant and animal.

os coxa (pl. os coxae). Same as innominate.

ossify. To become bone.

otoliths. Ear stones found in the crania of bony fish.

Passeriformes. Taxonomic order of perching birds.

pectoral rays. Bone of the fish skeleton's shoulder girdle.

pelvis (pl. pelves). Structure that includes the hip bones (innominates or os coxae), sacrum, and coccyx.

penultimate vertebrae. Next to last vertebra in a fish skeleton; has only one short spine.

Perciformes. Taxonomic order of perchlike fish.

Perissodactyls. Hoofed herbivores; have teeth that are adapted for grazing; have an odd number of toes.

perthotaxic. Relating to a process that limits the animals that can end up in an assemblage based on how the skeletons of animals have been altered at a given time and place.

pes. Bones of the foot.

phalanges. Finger and toe bones; they articulate with metacarpals or metatarsals or their equivalent.

pharyngeal teeth. Teeth that are located in the throat of a fish instead of in the jaws.

phylum. Taxonomic level between kingdom and class; this book is concerned with the phylum of Chordata.

pit features. Holes dug in the ground that become filled with trash over time.

plan. Looked at from above.

plastron. The lower shell of turtles and tortoises.

pleurodont. Having teeth that emerge from a single common groove in a jawbone.

postdepositional. After being deposited in the ground.

postclavicle. Bone of the fish skeleton's shoulder girdle.

posterior. Toward the back.

postsacral vertebrae. Vertebrae that occur after the sacrum or sacral vertebrae.

precaudal vertebrae. Vertebrae in fish that come before the tail (caudal) vertebrae; have transverse processes that extend from the sides of the vertebral body.

precise. Specific.

prehensile. Capable of grasping.

premolars. Teeth between canines and molars; complex crowns with only one root.

presacral vertebrae. Vertebrae that occur before the sacral vertebrae or sacrum, found in amphibians.

Primates. Taxonomic order that includes monkeys, apes, and gibbons.

process. A projection of bone that extends outward from a larger bone; projections often have their own name.

Procyonidae. Taxonomic family that includes raccoons.

profile. A drawing of something as seen from the side.

Prolagidae. Taxonomic family of Mediterranean giant pikas, not a generally accepted taxonomic group.

provenience. Origin; in this volume, the location from which a bone was recovered.

proximal. Situated near the top and center of a body; opposite of **distal**.

pubic symphysis. Place where the two pubis bones articulate with each other.

pubis (pl. pubes). The bone of the pelvis that projects medially from the acetabulum.

puncture wound. Type of bone break where there is a clear point of impact but little other damage.

pygostyle. Fused caudal vertebrae in birds; supports the tail feathers.

quill knobs. Bumps on the shaft of the ulna of birds.

radio-ulna. The fused radius and ulna as found in amphibians.

radius (pl. radii). One of the bones of the forearm; it articulates with the ulna, humerus, and carpals.

ramus (pl. rami). A branch of bone; the horizontal branch of the mandible that holds the teeth and the vertical branch of the mandible that connects it to the cranium.

relational database. A computer database that links types of data to each other to allow for more sophisticated data analysis.

Reptilia. Taxonomic class of reptiles.

residential species. Species of animals that live in a specific area year-round.

ribs. Bones of the chest cavity that articulate with the thoracic vertebrae.

richness. Number of categories, either taxonomic identification or skeletal element; used to describe your assemblage.

robust data. Useful data with many details.

rodent gnawing. Marks created when a rodent gnaws on a bone.

Rodentia. Taxonomic order of rodents; it is the largest mammalian taxonomic group.

root etching. Marks created when the acids of a plant root touch a bone.

Ruminantia. Animals with complex stomachs to process large amounts of grass; this group is a suborder, a level of taxonomy between order and family.

sacral vertebrae. Vertebrae of the pelvic girdle that often fuse to form a sacrum or part of a synsacrum.

sacrum (pl. sacra). Fused sacral vertebrae; part of the pelvic girdle.

Sarcopterygii. Taxonomic class of lobe-finned fishes.

savanna. Habitat of grassland with some scattered trees.

saw marks. Marks created when a saw is used to cut a bone; the form of a saw mark is determined by the type of saw used.

scan site. Area of bone that was scanned to measure its density.

scapula (pl. scapulae). Shoulder blade.

sciatic foramen. A foramen found on the pelvis of birds.

seasonality. Time of year or season in which a site was occupied.

secodont. Having bladelike teeth.

selenodont. Having teeth with ridges that surround cusps.

Semionotiformes. Taxonomic order of gars.

Serpentes. Taxonomic suborder of snakes.

sexual dimorphism. Difference in size between individuals of the same species that can be explained by the difference between male and female forms.

side. Determine whether a specimen represents the left or right of a paired skeletal element such as a femur.

skeletal element. A specific bone.

skull. A cranium and a mandible.

spines. Long thin projections of bone.

spinous process. The structure that projects outward from the neural arch for muscle attachment.

spiral fracture. Type of bone break with a diagonal appearance from twisting of the bone; this occurs only if the bone was broken when it was still moist or fresh.

spongy bone. Trabecular bone; interior bone that is woven into a spongelike pattern.

Squamata. Taxonomic order that includes lizards and snakes.

stepped fractures. Angular breaks of a bone; this occurs only if the bone was broken when it was dry.

sternum (pl. sterna). The front of the thorax, where the ribs meet in the center of the chest.

stratum. Layer of soil.

Strigiformes. Taxonomic order of owls.

styloid process. A process on the distal radius; common in species with prehensile hands.

Suidae. Taxonomic family of hogs and pigs.

Suinae. Omnivorous artiodactyls; this group is a suborder, a level of taxonomy between order and family.

sullegic. Process that limits the animals that can end up in an assemblage based on how researchers collected the bones at a given time and place.

sun bleaching. Taking on a lighter color after prolonged exposure to the sun; said of bones in this volume.

supraclavicle. Bone of the fish skeleton's shoulder girdle.

suprascapula. Extension of the scapula blade found in frogs and toads.

survivorship. Analysis of the bones that appear in a faunal assemblage to evaluate what, if any, destruction occurred and resulted in the elimination of other bones from the assemblage.

swampland. Habitat of wetland with woody vegetation.

symphysis. A simple articulation where two of the same bones come together, such as the pubic symphysis.

synsacrum. Lumbar and sacral vertebrae fused with the pelvis in birds.

taphic. Relating to the process that limits the animals that can end up in an assemblage based on how the skeletons of animals are altered after burial.

taphonomic signatures. Marks on or discoloration of the bone that can reveal the taphonomy of an assemblage.

taphonomy. Study of everything that happened to an animal from the time it died until the time it is described in a technical report; "laws of burial".

tarsals. Small and compact bones of the ankle.

tarsometatarsus. The tarsals and metatarsals fused into one bone; found in birds.

taxonomic group. Type of animal to which a bone belongs.

taxonomy. Organization of all living things based on similarities in their bodies and behavior.

Tayassuidae. Taxonomic family of peccaries.

Testudines. Taxonomic order of turtles and tortoises.

thanatic. Relating to the process that limits the animals that can end up in an assemblage based on what animals have been removed from the living population at a given time and place.

thecodont. Having teeth with roots that emerge from sockets in the jawbones.

thin-sectioned. Cut into very thin and flat cross-sections so that the internal architecture can be seen.

third trochanter. Projection of bone on the medial shaft of the femur, for muscle attachment.

thoracic vertebrae. Vertebrae of the thorax; articulate with the ribs.

thorax. Skeletal elements of the chest.

tibia (pl. tibiae). Bone of the lower limb; articulates with the femur, the fibula, and the tarsals.

tibiofibula (pl. tibiofibulae). The tibia and fibula fused into one bone; found in amphibians.

tibiotarsus. The tibia, fibula, and some carpals fused into one bone; found in birds.

tooth pits. Circular punctures of the bone surface made by pointed teeth while gnawing or carrying a bone.

total number of fragments (TNF). Same as **number of identified specimens (NISP)**.

trabeculae. The "support webs" that make up trabecular bone.

trabecular bone. Spongy bone, interior bone that is woven into a spongelike pattern.

trampling marks. Marks created when bone is rubbed against grit when stepped on by humans or animals.

transverse processes. The structures that project outward from the sides of the centrum or neural arch of a vertebra for muscle attachment.

trephic. Relating to the process that limits the animals that can end up in a faunal catalog or database based on how the bones were analyzed and curated.

trochlea. Pulley-shaped articulation.

trochlear notch. The concave articular surface of the proximal ulna that forms the cup of the hooklike articulation.

tubercle. A small, rounded projection of bone.

tuberosities. Rounded projections of bone.

ulna (pl. ulnae). Bone of the forearm; articulates with the radius, humerus, and carpals.

ultimate vertebra. Last vertebra in a fish skeleton; lacks spines but has support for the tail fin.

uncinate process. Process that extends caudally from the ribs of birds; gives a forked appearance to the rib.

ungulate. Hoofed animal.

unidentifiable bone. Bone that cannot be identified despite attempts to do so.

unidentified bone. Bone that has not been identified but may be with additional analysis.

urostyle. A structure located at the end of the spinal column in fish and amphibians.

Ursidae. Taxonomic family of bears.

ventral. Relating to the underside of a body when the body is in its normal anatomical position.

vertebrae. Neck or back bone; bones of the spinal column.

vertebral foramen. The main hole in vertebrae through which the spinal cord passes.

weathered bone. Bone that has been altered by varying environmental conditions.

wild. Relating to animals that have not been domesticated.

worked bone. Bone that has been used as a raw material.

References

Abe, Y., C. W. Marean, P. J. Nilssen, Z. Assefa, and E. C. Stone. 2002. The Analysis of Cutmarks on Archaeofauna: A Review and Critique of Quantification Procedures, and a New Image-Analysis GIS Approach. *American Antiquity* 67(4): 643–63.

Animal Diversity Web. University of Michigan Museum of Zoology. http://animaldiversity.org.

Beach, M. A., and C. S. Causey. 1984. Bone Artifacts from Arroyo Hondo Pueblo. In *The Faunal Remains from Arroyo Hondo Pueblo, New Mexico,* ed. R. W. Lang and A. H. Harris, 187–226. Santa Fe, NM: School of American Research Press.

Behrensmeyer, A. K. 1978. Taphonomic and Ecologic Information from Bone Weathering. *Paleobiology* 4(2): 150–62.

Betts, M. W., H. D. G. Maschner, C. D. Schou, R. Schlader, J. Holmes, N. Clement, and M. Smuin. 2010. Virtual Zooarchaeology: Building a Web-Based Reference Collection of Northern Vertebrates for Archaeofaunal Research and Education. *Journal of Archaeological Science* 38(4): 755.e1–755.e9.

Brown, C. L., and C. E. Gustafson. 1979. *A Key to Postcranial Skeletal Remains of Cattle/Bison, Elk, and Horse.* Reports of investigations no. 57. Pullman: Laboratory of Anthropology, Washington State University.

Cannon, D. Y. 1987. *Marine Fish Osteology: A Manual for Archaeologists.* Burnaby, B.C.: Archaeology Press, Simon Fraser University.

Clarke, J., and K. Kietzke. 1967. Paleoecology of the Lower Nodule Zone: Brule Formation in the Big Badlands of South Dakota. *Fieldiana: Geology Memoir* 5: 111–29.

Cohen, A., and D. Serjeantson. 1996. *A Manual for the Identification of Bird Bones from Archaeological Sites.* London: Archetype Publications.

Gilbert, B. M. 1990. *Mammalian Osteology.* Columbia: Missouri Archaeological Society.

———, L. D. Martin, and H. G. Savage. 1996. *Avian Osteology.* Columbia: Missouri Archaeological Society.

Gilchrist, R., and H. C. Mytum. 1986. Experimental Archaeology and Burnt Animal Bone from Archaeological Sites. *Circaea* 4(1): 29–38.

Grayson, D. K. 1984. *Quantitative Zooarchaeology: Topics in the Analysis of Archaeological Faunas.* Orlando, FL: Academic Press.

Gust, S. M. 1983. Problems and Prospects in Nineteenth-Century California Zooarchaeology. In *Forgotten Places and Things: Archaeological Perspectives on American History,* ed. A. E. Ward, 341–48. Albuquerque: Center for Anthropological Studies.

Haglund, W. D. 1997. Rodents and Human Remains. In *Forensic Taphonomy: The Postmortem Fate of Human Remains,* ed. W. D. Haglund and M. H. Sorg, 405–14. Boca Raton, FL: CRC Press.

Hales, L. S. J., and E. J. Reitz. 1992. Historical Changes in Age and Growth of Atlantic Croaker, *Micropogonias undulatus* (Perciformes: Sciaenidae). *Journal of Archaeological Science* 19(1): 73–99.

Hargrave, L. L. 1970. *Mexican Macaws: Comparative Osteology and Survey of Remains from the Southwest.* Anthropological papers of the University of Arizona no. 20. Tucson: University of Arizona Press.

Hillson, S. 1990. *Teeth.* Cambridge Manuals in Archaeology. Cambridge: Cambridge University Press.

———. 1996. *Mammal Bones and Teeth: An Introductory Guide to Methods of Identification.* London: Institute of Archaeology, University College.

Jones, J. K., and R. W. Manning. 1992. *Illustrated Key to Skulls of Genera of North American Land Mammals.* Lubbock: Texas Tech University Press.

Klein, R. G., and K. Cruz-Uribe. 1984. *The Analysis of Animal Bones from Archaeological Sites.* Chicago: University of Chicago Press.

Lam, Y. M., X. Chen, and O. M. Pearson. 1999. Intertaxonomic Variability in Patterns of Bone Density and the Differential Representation of Bovid, Cervid, and Equid Elements in the Archaeological Record. *American Antiquity* 64(2): 343–62.

Lam, Y. M., O. M. Pearson, C. W. Marean, and X. Chen. 2003. Bone Density Studies in Zooarchaeology. *Journal of Archaeological Science* 30(12): 1701–1708.

Lang, R. W., and A. H. Harris. 1984. *The Faunal Remains from Arroyo Hondo Pueblo, New Mexico: A Study in Short-Term Subsistence Change.* Santa Fe, NM: School of American Research Press.

Lyman, R. L. 1994. *Vertebrate Taphonomy.* Cambridge Manuals in Archaeology. Cambridge: Cambridge University Press.

———. 2008. *Quantitative Paleozoology.* Cambridge Manuals in Archaeology. Cambridge: Cambridge University Press.

Monks, G. G. 1981. Seasonality Studies. In *Advances in Archaeological Method and Theory,* ed. M. J. Schiffer, vol. 4: 177–240. New York: Academic Press.

Morey, D. F., W. E. Klippel, and B. L. Manzano. 1991. Estimation of Live Weight of Fish Recovered from Archaeological Sites. In *Beamers, Bobwhites, and Blue-Points: Tributes to the Career of Paul W. Parmalee,* ed. J. R. Purdue, W. E. Klippel, and B. W. Styles, 91–98. Springfield: Illinois State Museum.

Novecosky, B. J., and P. R. W. Popkin. 2005. Canidae Volume Bone Mineral Density Values: An Application to Sites in Western Canada. *Journal of Archaeological Science* 32: 1677–90.

Oates, D. W., E. D. Boyd, and J. S. Ramaekers. 2003. *Identification of Waterfowl Breastbones and Avian Osteology (Sterna) of North American Anseriformes.* Special publication no. 10. Martinsville: Virginia Museum of Natural History.

Olsen, S. J. 1964. *Mammal Remains from Archaeological Sites.* Papers of the Peabody

Museum of Archaeology and Ethnology, vol. 56, no. 1. Cambridge, MA: Peabody Museum, Harvard University.

———. 1968. *Fish, Amphibian, and Reptile Remains from Archaeological Sites.* Papers of the Peabody Museum of Archaeology and Ethnology, vol. 56, no. 2. Cambridge, MA: Peabody Museum, Harvard University.

———. 1979. *Osteology for the Archaeologist.* Papers of the Peabody Museum of Archaeology and Ethnology, vol. 56, nos. 3–5. Cambridge, MA: Peabody Museum, Harvard University.

———. 1982. *An Osteology of Some Maya Mammals.* Papers of the Peabody Museum of Archaeology and Ethnology, vol. 73. Cambridge, MA: Harvard University Press.

Pacheco Torres, V. R., A. A. Enciso, and E. G. Porras. 1986. *The Osteology of the South American Camelids.* Archaeological Research Tools, vol. 3. Los Angeles: University of California Institute of Archaeology.

Pavao, B., and P. W. Stahl. 1999. Structural Density Assays of Leporid Skeletal Elements with Implications for Taphonomic, Actualistic, and Archaeological Research. *Journal of Archaeological Science* 26(1): 53–66.

Reitz, E. J., and E. S. Wing. 2008. *Zooarchaeology,* 2nd ed. Cambridge Manuals in Archaeology. Cambridge: Cambridge University Press.

Romer, A. S. 1956. *Osteology of the Reptiles.* Chicago: University of Chicago Press.

Schmid, E. 1972. *Atlas of Animal Bones. For Prehistorians, Archaeologists, and Quaternary Geologists.* Amsterdam, NY: Elsevier.

Seafross, G. 1995. *Skulls and Bones: A Guide to the Skeletal Structures and Behavior of North American Mammals.* Mechanicsburg, PA: Stackpole.

Serjeantson, D. 2009. *Birds.* Cambridge Manuals in Archaeology. Cambridge: Cambridge University Press.

Silver, I. A. 1963. The Aging of Domestic Animals. In *Science in Archaeology: A Survey of Progress and Research,* ed. D. Brothwell and E. Higgs, 283–302. New York: Praeger.

Smith, G. S. 1979. *Mammalian Zooarchaeology, Alaska: A Manual for Identifying and Analyzing Mammal Bones from Archaeological Sites in Alaska.* Anthropology and Historic Preservation, Cooperative Park Studies Unit. Occasional Paper no. 18. Fairbanks: University of Alaska.

Sobolik, K. D., and D. G. Steele. 1996. *A Turtle Atlas to Facilitate Archaeological Identifications.* Mammoth Site of Hot Springs, SD, in conjunction with the Office of Research and Public Services, University of Maine.

Stahl, P. W. 1999. Structural Density of Domesticated South American Camelid Skeletal Elements and the Archaeological Investigation of Prehistoric Andean Ch'arki. *Journal of Archaeological Science* 26(11): 1347–68.

Walker, R. 1985. *A Guide to Post-Cranial Bones of East African Animals.* Norwich, Eng.: Hylochoerus Press.

Index

pelvic girdle
overview, 70–71
amphibians, 37, 38f, 52, 71f
birds, 51, 74
class distinctions summarized, 75
fish, 49, 74
mammals, 24f, 47–48, 71–72, 73f
reptiles, 52, 74–75, 78
penis bone, 101f, 102
penultimate vertebrae, fish, 64
Perciforme order, 25, 35
percussion-based fractures, 104, 105f
Perissodactyla order, 25, 26–28, 72, 98
See also horse bones
permit requirements, carcass collection,
42
personality, assemblage, 7–8
perthotaxic process, defined, 11
phalanges
overview, 79, 88, 96–97
amphibians, 52, 88
birds, 83, 88
mammals, 48, 88, 94f
reptiles, 52, 88
Phasianus colchicus
limb bones, 21f, 80f, 89f
pelvic girdle, 71f
shoulder girdle, 76f
vertebrae, 60f, 65f
pheasants, in taxonomic order, 36
Phyllomedusa sauvagii
limb bones, 38f, 80f, 89f
pelvic girdle, 71f
shoulder girdle, 76f
pig bones
age indicators, 24f
limbs, 24f, 80
metapodials, 96
pelvic girdle, 24f
sex indicators, 101
teeth, 29
twisted characteristic, 30
vertebrae, 47
pigeon bones, 36f, 139
pigs, 28, 44
pikas, 31
pit features, in contextual analysis, 136
plastrons, Testudines order, 40, 52

pleurodont teeth, 38–39
postclavicle ray, fish, 77
posterior position, defined, 52–53
postsacral vertebrae, amphibians, 52
precaudal vertebrae, fish, 49, 63–64
premolars, 26–27, 32, 57
preparation of assemblage
overview, 7–8, 15
cleaning, 8–9
mending, 12–15
sorting, 10–12
presacral vertebrae, amphibians, 51
pressure test, bones, 12
Primate order, 25, 32, 72
Procyonidae family, teeth, 101
Procyon lotor, baculum, 101f
Prolagidae family, 31
pronghorn antelope, 28
provenience-based analysis, importance,
7–8
proximal position
overview, 52–53
data field for, 123
metapodials, 94, 95–98
proximal position, limb bones
amphibians, 87
birds, 85–86, 92, 93
mammals, 79, 80–81, 83, 88–91
reptiles, 87, 93
universal characteristic, 88
pubis
amphibians, 52
birds, 51, 74
mammals, 24f, 48, 71, 72
reptiles, 52, 74–75
puncture wounds, bones, 104, 105f
pygostyle, birds, 51, 64–65
Python regius, 25f, 60f, 66f

quail, in taxonomic order, 36
quantity calculations, assemblage,
129–133, 138
quill knobs, birds, 85–86

rabbit bones, 31–32, 91, 98
raccoon baculum, 101f
radio-ulna, amphibians, 52, 79–80,
87–88